Just The Typical American Negro

Jun & Louise Briggs-DeHorney

authorHOUSE®

AuthorHouse™
1663 Liberty Drive
Bloomington, IN 47403
www.authorhouse.com
Phone: 1-800-839-8640

First published by AuthorHouse 10/27/2009

ISBN: 978-1-4389-9381-2 (sc)
ISBN: 978-1-4490-3065-0 (hc)

Library of Congress Control Number: 2009909868

Printed in the United States of America
Bloomington, Indiana

This book is printed on acid-free paper.

DEDICATION:

This book is dedicated to all the Author brothers and sisters of all walks of life, throughout the Universe. We are all brothers and sisters by blood. Can we stop the killing? And think of only love and peace, sure we can that will be the birth of harmony peace and love be upon you.

The Author and the Co Author Jun & Louise DeHorney

FOUR REASONS WHY YOU SHOULD READ THE BOOK

1. To widen ones' scope

2. To broaden one's horizon.

3. Learn to develop one's mind set

4. Gain wisdom from the unknown

TABLE OF CONTENTS

TOM THOMPSON TOPP
BETTER KNOWN AS LITTLE TRIPLE T'.

Thinking is the most important is the most important element of any mind therefore, one should always think.

As the writer's father would say, one should not be without their thinking cap since, you are what you think. And the most important factor is to choose what to think, since the mind is what make the person. The mind educates every component of one's body without a sound mind one can very well say, it only matter taking up space.

The writer grandfather was born Tom Thompson Topp he called himself little triple T, since he was 5'7 and weigh 130 pounds and people describe him as being very arrogant. He would describe himself as being smarter than the average dumb ass, he would boast about how he could out work any big man. Saying he done more work by 8a.m. than the average person did all day. He was born in Pine Bluff Arkansas in 1883, and he ran away from home in 1896, he was the father of the writer's mother Josephine by 1900. He died in 1922, at the ripe old age of thirty nine as we write he is still credited for being the wealthiest Negro in fannin County Texas. He would boast about how he had the same materials as the white folks.

Likes, his three hundred plus acres of land was self contained. And he was the first Negro in Fannin County to have land adjoining wealthy white folks he could read and write at six years old. He spoke three different languages French, Spanish, and English and would boast and tell other Negroes that they were so dumb, that they wouldn't know their name if they seem it walking down the road.

He would go to the white market in Ravenna Texas and drink water out of the white folk's dipper, when the white man approach to tell him and the writer will quote him "Tom you know that is the white man bucket and dipper you Niggers can go outside and drink water out of the horse's trough". "Tom would reply jump on me and

1

can't fight". The white man would reply Tom you will do this too many times.

History has plainly demonstrated that wisdom is more valuable than gold, little triple T. died from being poison. Poison was placed inside the white folks water bucket at the old age of thirty nine it was said, that the water bucket was placed at the front with a sign on the bucket that read Tom Topp only as a reminder to other Negroes not to duplicate his act. After Tom death Negroes made up a song that bought sense was better than free sense any day. One would only guess O. J. could contest to that.

Little triple T's. Father was described as a white African to this day the writer don't know what that means, the writer can only wonder. But it was said, that little triple T, father spoke five languages. Just before the start of the civil war he was caught by the Slave patrol in New Orleans he told the Slave patrol that he wasn't a Slave their reply was you are just a high yellow nigger with curly hair. He worked during the Civil war on the Mississippi as a ship steward, may peace be upon his soul.

THIS IS TO ALERT THE READER:

The Author is the second generation born out of Slavery, the second to attend school, the first generation to graduate from high school. Therefore, the Author intellect derived from the roots that were available but, the Author is very grateful and thankful for existing in this here America. The Author great- grandfather E.L. who was a former Slave owner said it best's that the Negro, despite their traumatic experience was one thousand percent better off here in America than they would have been if they were left in their native land, running wild and naked. And nobody knows the America Negro better than the master, that was only one half of the mix, and the Author's other grandfather who's name was Johansson Topp. Who was the father of little triple T. Who was the father of the Author's mother Josephine, Josephine said her father said they were given the last name because Topp because they were the top dog, the name derived from England. Johansson Topp was put into Slavery for speaking broken English but came to this here America as a free man from England.

We the writer will spare you the reader the details because this book is about the typical American Negro

Hope you enjoy the reading.

The picture above is Josephine Topp DeHorney this was Tom Thompson Topp pride and joy. Tom put the label of precious, on Josie she never knew what hard work was. She never knew suffering, she just believe that someday this will all be over.

She passed into the great begun at the age of 97, her last twenty Years of her life she was blind just as the writer. The last 14 Years of her life she spent in a nursing home, she learned what it was to suffer. She was born with a label and 'oh' how she tried to live up to that label. She was blessed with a very brilliant mind, but by that label that was restored upon her mind went to a belief, a belief of what she wanted. Her father little tripe T' ran away from home at 13, thought he had an imagination of what he wanted. Suffering from inexperience was a proud father at seventeen. Married Jose's mother who had a 2 Year old son by a previous affair, as we write Tom was credited for owning more land than any Negro in Fannin County Texas He died at age 39 at the hands of not knowing not knowing that the mouth was a powerful weapon. There wasn't any pictures that existed of Tom all we can do is wonder that's the trademark of the American Negro. Not knowing still exists for the Negro none Tom's survivals knew that one had to have an imagination for what they wanted for the future. And from that fact and that fact alone displays the irony of ignorance that exists for the family.

Since all families derive from the genetics, no one had the imagination to mark Tom grave not even his precious daughter Josephine. All Josie could say, he was buried by a tree, the writer remembers his mother Josie arguing with her first cousin ex-Slave Ruben Phillips son. The son said his mother was buried in the spot that Josie said Tom was buried, and the beats goes on the American Negro is just a wonderer.

One of Tom parable was one has to tell the ignorant Negro everything even what, when, how, and why that includes religion. That was Tom parable as Tom would say, I didn't tell them to mark my grave with a stone they are only Negroes. And all Negroes have a developmental problem; it seems to be that way that's the typical American Negro.

LITTLE TIDBITS ABOUT THE CO -AUTHOR:

Louise Briggs --- DeHorney is a Sociology and historian. She has been instrumental in implementing a comprehensive projects for students to participate in an array of things to celebrate black history month and through out the year. Ranging from research papers, art work and drama in order to make sure each individual student that she associate with have a complete understanding of the importance of our Negro History. In addition, she is president of E.M.M.A.D. educated minorities making a difference. My Philosophy is to strive to be the best therefore, excellent will be in reach and by being educated one will be headed in the right direction. Too many young people are headed toward a dead end street and sooner or later they will come to a crossroad, and it's the choice they make, and that choice will determine their future down the road.

The Co- Author obtained her degree besides, maintaining her role as a wife, mother, full time worker, and carrying 18 hours back to back but that didn't stop her from making the Dean's list. This is something that she is very proud of considering the ridicule she receive while growing up as a child in Beirne Arkansas. Our family went through a lot of hard times; nevertheless, we made it through all of them.

Some of the people that the Co-Author grew - up with were portrayed to be so much smarter than the Co-Author and always said they were going to attend College but it never happen. The writer was made to feel alienated, which brought about shyness and inferiority toward other people.

The Co -Author said that in order to say this, the Author's father had a saying and it goes like this the race is not given to the swift,

But to the one who endures to the end. That reminds the Co-Author of the rabbit and the tortoise the story is self explanatory, which mean follow your dreams and desires and see where they lead you.

The Co- Author is the only one out of seven siblings to attend College or earn a degree. She has a degree in Sociology from the University of Arkansas @ Little Rock. She came from a small Country and it was more like a jungle than anything else called Beirne Arkansas. So remember it doesn't matter where you come from, it only matters where one is going.

In Addition, a special appreciation goes out too the following people:

The writer's wife and Co Author Louise Briggs---- De Horney for her support and dedication. The writer's father Julion DeHorney for his support, Josephine Top DeHorney for her advice. Emma Jean Sweet--- DeHorney Mr. Charlie Hill, Jesse Hill, Coach Russell Tracy, Coach Clifford Bryant, Mr. Bohannon, Monroe Morrison, Sam Brown, Carl Gilmore, Clarence Gilmore, J.D. Gilmore, Aaron Jones, Al Finn, Harry Harris, Zorro Foley, Curly Culp, Shirley Culp, Mr. Walter Briggs, Guthrie Tate Briggs her favorite parable was I don't' care don't have a home. Lee Olive Savage, Walter Cunningham, Sr., Elmer Lee, Jesse Nunn, Dr. Clinton Harvey, Lee Dale Muldrew, John Harmon, Nathan Tidwell, all of these people have contribute to the elevation of the writer's mental component, and this is the writer way of saying thanks.

May peace be upon you?
Jun Yellow Dog DeHorney

As there are too many people to list all of them such as Thomas {peek sight} Hines, Willie {chili} Meeks, Thaddeus {T. G.} Gipson.

Gratitude of thanks for people who contributed to the being of the writer as we write.

The writer would like to give a very special thanks to his great grandfather; this may come as a surprise to many since the great-grandfather was a Slave owner. And was the beginning roots of the American Negro known as the DeHorney's the great grand father Ebenezer Lafayette Dohoney 'yes' the writer know the name is spelled two different ways, that is an inherited trait. At the time of Ebenezer creation, the creation was property, property did not require a last name. But once the so- called freedom was declared all Negroes had to have a last name.

Hanneh was the original Slave; she was the one that gave birth to the writer's grandfather sired by Ebenezer. So when freedom was declared it was said that Ebenezer gave Hanneh a piece of paper with her name, the writer grandfather name but who knows for sure what was on the paper. Since Hanneh couldn't read or her son William, neither had spent one day of their life in school, they had to be taught how to make a mark. One letter means everything in writing not knowing is the most dangerous position on the Universe. It has been documented that the writer's name itself has been spelled many different ways. For example, Dehoney, Dehourney, and Dehorney that's a choice and from that choice a decision has to come.

The writer's father was the first generation to attend school, he mastered that with a third grade education, and the writer was the second generation to attend school.

Thanks to the laws of this here America and the position of the poor old Negro the Dehorney's a beginning begins, it can be described as a behavior disorder and the beats goes on. But the writer does not hold a grudge but the writer do believe that truth will set one free but one must surrender to truth in order to be enlighten by wisdom. Since wisdom, is the main ingredient in a structure no structure, no wisdom it's that simple my friends as the writer great grandmother would say give every dog its due. This Ebenezer Lafayette Do honey {1832-1919} was a college graduate and the valedictorian of his class graduated form the University of Louisville with a law degree. He practice law in Paris Texas thirty five miles from the point where the Dehorney's generation derived from. He was a Judge and a State Senator, ran for Governor in the great State of Texas, and was mention for a candidate for the president of this here America. He was one the original signees of the State constitution of Texas the one that governs Texas as we write. This is an abbreviated portion of his resume; the writer read one of his eighteen books that he wrote. By reading the Constitution of man it not only enlighten the writer it inspired the writer and gave him a since of belonging. It gave the writer a new spiritual beginning to how, where, and why The Negro exists, thanks E. L. for a job well done we will always be with you in spirit. I forgave you for my eye disease may peace be upon your soul, 'yes' E.L. is buried in Paris Texas in a segregated cemetery for white's only. But his blood is still running warm in the veins of many, as Hanneh would say give all dogs their due.

Would you America agree?

THE WRITER GRATITUDE OF APPRECIATION:

The first appreciation goes to you the reader, thanks to you in advance: and a special thanks goes to my lovely wife Louise Briggs -- DeHorney This fate would not be possible without Louise she is my ears and eyes she and I are veterans of 44 Years as we write

Another special thanks to a very special family friend, of 55 Years as we write Mr. Charlie Hill who is as we write 94 years old. He is the prime example of love, if anyone was ever made in the image of the supreme master whom some people refer to as God it is Mr. Charlie Hill. One could just call him Charlie do good Hill, or Charlie given Hill if it was ever a brother man it was and is Mr. Hill. If there is a heaven that exists above his spot is reserved and waiting he was and is a living angel. His deed is to numerous to mention, it's a book by itself; his seed was always planted in his deed. One of his favorite parables was and is just keep doing well for others. The only time the writer seen him angry was when someone was not trying to do something for self.

Mr. Hill was always there for whatever the task was whether it was pulling someone out of the mud hole, ploughing one garden, giving one food, providing one with shelter, helping one find a summer job, rescuing one livestock or giving one encouragement. It seemed no was not in his vocabulary, thanks Mr. Hill even though hope is worthless. We do hope you reach your grandfather age of a hundred and six, keep on trying, and please keep on keeping on, may peace be upon you.

Before starting and writing this book the writer thought just existing in Fannin County Texas would be the hardest and compelling fate that alone would ever encounter. Despite the fact training and trying to exist as an athlete and training two sons to be athletes. Having over twenty fights as a fighter driving over two million miles as a tractor-- trailer driver, working 27 hours straight, and driving nine hundred miles without a break this book tops it all.

Despite losing the writer eyesight in the process, despite warning from the doctors the writer perseveres onward. There are two things the writer hates, that is loosing and ignorance, that's the very reason why the writer wrote this book. The writer would like to think of it as a seed in a deed to sum it up best, as to get a understanding where the writer derived from we will go all the way back to Bonham Texas, and use a statement from his formal Washington high school classmate Elbert White and I quote "Jun you know I don't go back to Fannin County that much because when I go visit or even talk to someone from Fannin County it gives a bad since of smell or taste in my system. It take me as least six months to get it out of my system, it's the same as I first remembered it no progress, that's why everyone that were eager for change fled".

Elbert White.

The writer cried while writing this book; sadden by the facts of reality while thanking the past members of the Negro race for paving the way that exist for today's Negroes may peace be upon their soul. The hardest part the writer had to deal with was trying to get pictures of people to help develop this book, no Charlie Hill effect here. So in essence, Mr. Hill is advance beyond his time just look at his resume because the writer was promise but the delivery was not made its as though the writer doesn't exist. It's like a writer is some type of super freak from outer space, and having problems with delusions. That derives from ignorance thanks for nothing may peace are upon you.

It takes all kind to make the typical American Negro even nothing. It seems as the poor old Negro is still hoping that nothing creates something, to conclude this, formal middle weight champion Jermain Taylor said it best I am so proud of myself for this book.

THE REASON WHY THE AUTHOR WROTE THE BOOK:

The main reason why the writer wrote this book is because the author had the opportunity to talk without being interrupted; it was the freedom of talking without interruption. The writer grew up in an environment where everyone had the custom of talking at the same time, no one listen, the writer had the perception that everyone knew except the writer. It seemed that in the environment the writer derived from only the environment listen to the preacher or white America. After evaluating the preacher, the writer came to the conclusion, that the writer had more enlightenment than the preacher and white America just serve as an authority figure. The writer was interested in expressing himself so, what better way it is to express one self than to write, so here we are.

Throughout the writer life the writer had no one to express too, the writer was always rejected even by the writer's parents and siblings. It seemed as all the writer idea logics were wrong, raised in the Country until sixteen years of age, at sixteen moves to a large town and given a mop and a bucket, and was told to seek his fortune. As if this was better than a hoe and a cotton sack, didn't have the opportunity to live a normal teenage life. The writer told his brother that he was giving up his mop and bucket to try out for the basketball team his senior year in high school.

Despite the writer was 6'2 a hundred and ninety pounds including a 32 inch waist he was considered fat by his siblings, despite the fact the writer had no basketball experience except for the play ground.

The writer brother said I was stupid for given up a mop and a broom for a hope and that I would never make the team. By the laws of reality, he was the prince of darkness not only did the writer make the team, he made the first team and he gain enough experience to teach his son the game. And his son went on to gain a scholarship for a free education and to earn two degrees and is a basketball Coach himself.

So, the writer said that in order to say this just because someone rejects one, that is not a conclusion history has plainly demonstrated that, Michael Jordon was once the victim of rejection so, stand up and fight, believe in self, light comes after darkness.

A Contribute to a warrior and a dear friend Tommy and Dennis {Doff} White:

Tommy was the daughter of little triple T, and the sister of the writer's mother Josephine. If ever a couple were ever compatible Tommy and Doff were very compatible, by just talking to them one could very easily understand that they had a fifty- fifty mix. It can't get any better than that, Doff derived from the descendents of the African, the red man, and white America. One can very well see African descent on his picture. Very often white America mix will lie dormant, on the outside because of the power of the African dormancy. But if one knows the roots of their history, they will know that Doff mother was a Gentry, and that is history within itself. It seems as though as if Doff and Tommy was finger printed by love. From the first time the writer remembers them to the last, they were the same that is a result of surrending to truth.

Every human is born of ignorance, so the human mind is educated by association, that association derive from one's environment and community, and Ravenna Texas was no different.

The writer's root goes back to Ravenna Texas so by that fact and that fact alone stimulates the reality of the writer soul. By those stimulations the writer had a choice and from that choice derives a habit, and from that habit ones develop ones' character.

Doff and Tommy always displayed positive character as the writer's father would say every now and then one will find a traveler.

The writer's father was talking about the god of love and peace? Or we talking about the God of evil and destruction.

The writer cannot forget what Tommy and Doff meant to the writer for instance; the writer had never eaten homemade hamburgers as a child until he ate Tommy's. It was as if the only place one could get hamburgers was from white America in other words, what the Negro called store bought, 'man' when this aunt Tommy would feed you, you could see the gravitation in her, it would be as if life was exploding. As a child every Saturday night the writer would want to go to this Aunt Tommy's house for a good hamburger, man how the writer still loves hamburgers as we write. As we writer writes the writer still have to cook hamburgers that is homemade at least once a week, whether or not he need them or not.

So, the writer can just say from the fruits of love Aunt Tommy spirit lives on that is love my friends. One can very well say the writer had not forgotten were he came from and from that impact the writer wanted to be like Tommy and Doff by showing love.

For instance, when the writer's niece and nephew Scharlene and Mike mother left them, they were sent to Texas too live with the writer mother and father so, by association the writer could only do what he was program to do and that was to offer a hand of love, to Scharlene and mike. Therefore, every Saturday night the writer would cook hamburgers for the whole family, and not once, has this Scharlene or Mike said thanks. In fact, they don't even call the writer, and this Scharlene has a master degree in education, reality teaches one that education don't make the person the mind is what make the person. This here Scharlene once told the writer that she didn't hold on to the past, the writer is still wondering since the Negro is a wonderer.

What kind of intoxication was she smoking or taking? Was she telling the writer the education she obtained was to no avail? That's why one obtain an education is to hold on too what one have gain by learning.

Aunt Tommy once told the writer when one get something good, hold on to it and use it as an endowment. Can that explain if one doesn't know where they come from how can they know where they are going? Is that the poor old Negroes nomadic innateness? The mind is what makes the person from that actuality this Tommy White call the writer to let the writer know his older brother had died.

As the poor old Negro would say, birds of a feather flop together and history has demonstrated by association, association will affect one's mind positive or negative the choice is up to the individual whether that individual will let that association impact their life. That will depend on that individual mental acceptance, acceptance meaning the individual have a choice of what they let enter their mental capacity. Meaning, one is what they think and one have a choice of what to think and from that choice which derives one's character the mind is what make the person. And this Doff White was the same American who built two houses and uses little triple T's land for an endowment he didn't wonder off to the city even though he was used as a human machine. Doff once told the writer that he would walk ten miles one way just to break rocks to build roads for white America. When in fact Doff had to what the poor old Negro would describe as mud- in and out of their community in order to get to the white community. Because the Negro community was still in its original primitive state of existence from sun -up to can't see six days a week and Doff would go to church on Sunday. He would knell down and pray giving thanks for what he had now, that's love my friends no one has to ask what God he served because it's plain and simple it was the love of God, and that love of God is truth. Ones' principle will surely surrender to reality; he was a man among men.

So many men have left their children to take care of someone else's children. Because they are wonderers which, derive from their founding fathers so thanks Tommy and Doff for the friendship of love.

Your spirit lives on May peace be upon your soul forever, and forever is a long time.

THE PRETENSE OF A PERFECT NEGRO:

Little triple T, once said people come in three different forms and the poor old Negro is no different it's only a different scenario. A scenario that no one can duplicate it's for Negroes only little triple T, said one will set and do nothing the writer will call him Johnny dumb ass. And here is another person who is all wrap up in self, he will be called slick Eugene, and last and not least here is the person who want to conquer the world we will name him captain know it all. These are actual people, but their identity is protected one will think that everyone want something but there is only one problem people has to be taught how to obtained

Not knowing is the most dangerous position on the Universe, and history has plainly demonstrated that position is the most important spot on the Universe. The poor old Negro is a created race, America is all the poor old Negro know, they know nothing about Africa in essence, and the poor old Negro only knows what white America have programmed them with. The poor old Negro can be compared to a blank role of film one can take a picture on a blank role of film but that role of film is nothing until one develops it.

At this point, the writer cannot go forward without describing to you the reader about this real life character that represent this here America's typical Negro, his code name is slick Eugene. He was born in a very small north Texas town the house he was born in, one could see everything in town from the that house, including the cotton fields his father labored in.

At the age of ten, Eugene moved to the largest town in north Texas right down on the red river. Dallas was one hundred miles to the south of this town. This town was so large, that one could get lost but was large enough to have paved streets and lights for the white folks. But the poor old Negro still had Nigger conditions no street lights and no paved roads, the only thing different from the Country are that the Negroes had rock roads and a Negro doctor.

Up until this point, Eugene didn't even know that any doctor existed but Eugene would go on to say he seen a need to better his conditions so, he obtained a job as a shoe shine boy at a Hotel at five cents a whop according to Eugene within ten days, he was the best shoe shine boy in the State of Texas. One have to understand, that Eugene didn't even know that any Doctor existed So, he obtained a job as a shoe shine boy at a hotel at five cent a whop One has to understand, that Eugene was the second of four siblings and he was the one that had a label restored up on him. The label would read as follows: A leader, the smartest, the one with the best idea logics, sense he was light skin and curly headed it was natural he was the best looking boy in Texas bar none.

So at the raw age of ten slick Eugene became the hardest working ten year old in north Texas. He would often laugh and say, he would shine shoes for a nickel and tap dance for a dime even though his dancing ability was question. Because the writer have never heard of anyone seeing him dance not even his mother. Eugene would go on to claim at twelve years of age that he clean -up a two story office complex all by himself. A claim that could not be sustained by his mother she would neither confirm, nor deny that fate. She would go on to say, that he came home late at night and would have money the question remains if the office building really existed. At thirteen he was in the 8th grade and was the best lineman on the varsity football team in high school. He only stood 5'6 and a hundred and thirty pounds he profess to be the best offense tackle ever to play the game in north Texas. He proclaim to have off set his size by throwing sand and spitting in the opponent eyes, at thirteen his older brother said he ran away from home to be found in town at the yellow house about thirty miles away. A yellow house is a termed used by white America to describe a hoe house it was for light skins Negro women and white males only and no black women allowed. His father heard he was thirty miles away in another town after working six days on the rail road a job for Niggers only on his day of rest which was Sunday the father walked thirty miles to retrieve slick Eugene.

After retrieving slick Eugene, he and his father walked thirty miles back home and Monday morning the father was back during his duty on the rail road tracks. The writer would like to point out this is a fact not a fabrication it was said that Eugene was down at the buzzard nest which was a corner specified for Negroes only. Eugene was hustling up business from the white man who would come to the buzzer nest looking for Negro women. Eugene was hustling customers for the yellow house just to get to sleep with his favorite lady, who was five years, his elder. At sixteen slick Eugene who said he was so smart in school he got double promoted twice that was also questionable since he was thirteen in the eight grade. At sixteen he was a senior in high school and he was in a battle for valedictorian He persuaded his father to sign the papers so he could enter the armed forces Eugene would later claimed the real reason why he went to the army he was associating with this rich white woman. She had falling in love with him and he had to get out of town during this time Eugene would also say, that six white boys jump him in a white neighborhood and beat him up. The following night Eugene said he retrieve an ice pick from the wall and went looking for the white boys and he found each white boy all six of them and stab each one six times. Eugene said he wore gloves and a ski mask to protect his identity he would go on to say it made the morning news paper. The head lines read mask wearing night stalker attack six white boys. Slick Eugene would say that was the pay back for his beating he said he wash the ice pick off and poke it back into the wall as though it was never removed. Back in the day most Negroes didn't have a refrigerator, most didn't have electricity. So, an ice pick was common to break up ice they had bought from the ice man, so they would just slam the ice pick back into the wall.

Also, during Eugene life he lay claim to have run a repair shoe shop all by his lonesome, for what it is worth. Eugene served three years in the Army and he claimed he learned how to drive a truck in the Army. He once told his sister, he was so good at what he did he did not sleep with the enlisted men. He slept with a lieutenant for what it is worth.

Upon leaving the Army, he came back to north Texas and finish high school although, Eugene claims he had the credits and all he had to do was just walk in and get his diploma. He forsaken that fate just for the experience now, from the this time he renewed his acquaintance at the yellow house. He also journeyed to Chicago, and when he left he told his mother he was going to be a shoe cobbler. Once he returned after a ninety day stay, he would tell people that he went to Chicago to attend the University of Chicago. University of Chicago to be a college professor, but once he arrived he found out that a hustler made more money than a college professor. Since he was a natural hustler, there was no need to study so, he returned back to north Texas by now his family had moved back to the country.

Since Eugene had no base, he moved in with them and went to work on a country farm having no car Eugene went from hustling in Chicago to just hustling a ride nine miles from the country to town to see his favorite lady. By now the events of time had changed with his favorite lady the yellow house had been closed down and his favorite lady had gotten married. His favorite lady and her husband were walking down the road one evening when they ran into one of her former paying gents. Then an argument began the ex-gent pulled out a knife and deliberately cut her husband to pieces. Needless to say, slick Eugene went and married his favorite lady at the age of twenty -one for what? It is still being deliberated among the people, because she was a large woman and bigger than Eugene. She was light skin and hair hung down her back but had a face and nose as any ex- fighter would despise should the writer say any more.

THE CONSEQUENCE OF A PRETENSE

The people tell a story, on how Eugene tried to lead his people to a better world Eugene, Johnny dumb ass, and captain no it all was trying to escape the horror and terror of being a poor Negro living in the south. So, they all left and began to walk they were going north looking for a better life. They walked for two days through the woods following the leadership of Eugene and he said there must be a better life some where So they came up on a rail road track, none of the pack knew what a railroad track was Johnny dumb ass sure didn't know because he was just dumb captain know it all just wanted to know but didn't know but slick Eugene was the man he had to know so he would just tell them anything because they were looking for him for leadership.

He had to deliver so he told them the track was a trail to the city, Eugene was just talking and telling then how they could follow the track to the city and would say man you have to learn when you don't know you have to follow someone who does. So follow me and I will take you there Eugene was in the lead in the middle of the track, as if he was some type of chief. Captain knows it all was to his right and close to the edge of the track, Johnny dumb ass was the same to the left of Eugene. Johnny dumb ass heard something. And looked around and saw a train just a coming and he hollered something is coming so Johnny dumb ass jump out of the way, Captain know it all jump to the right then wrapped up in self slick Eugene didn't move. It is not known if the engineer of the train saw them or not because the poor old Negro have a saying that the American Negro is so small that white America cannot identify with them. And white America have a saying its only a Nigger so run over them and make them part of the environment. By that the writer do not know the facts of this case but for sure, Johnny dumb ass and captain know it all, latched on to the train as it was rolling by both rode to success and slick Eugene legends lives on. Someone said they saw him putting his mop bucket in a corner hung his broom up on the wall and took the vacuum cleaner off his back for the last time three months short of his seventy ninth birthday hump over, one eyed, without a will or a purpose in life other than that of a servant and still trying to find a reject that someone else had rejected still professing to be the greatest chef in America that is the way it is for the one who is wrap up in self . After un- wrapping themselves they will find they are very small they will always talk about what I was not what I am that person like slick Eugene is like little Ruby husband. Little Ruby who is less than five feet tall and weigh less than 90 lbs went out and married a 6'8 guy and weigh 400 pounds who whip her three times a day and twice on Sunday whether she needed it or not and Ruby would pray that the lord would removed her pain and once her husband climbed on top of the house to repair the roof once he repaired the roof he was coming down off the roof he slip and fell his head, landed in a open window the window fell shut on his neck killed him dead as a nail. Ruby would say it was God's help sent from above the Lord answered her prayers Once he arrived at the mortuary they found out they didn't have a casket to fit him so they called Ruby and asked her what are we going to do with him Ruby replied give him an enema and bury him in a shoe box. Iron site is a virtue, what was Ruby thinking while they were making the four babies that he left behind? What was Ruby thinking while they were setting smoking crack and drinking the white man liquor? Since Ruby is what she thinks and Ruby is the one who chooses what to think Ruby have not develop, the equipment to understand that the mind is what make the person that's the typical American Negro my friends.

THE CREATION OF A CONSEQUENCE FOR THE NEGRO

As with any machine, the machine requires a maker the servant or mortar is no different.

The poor old America Negro was created to serve as a servant or mortar, for this here America. The American Negro is a cross between the black African and any other race that was free to come to America and purchase a African for the duties of a mortar.

Despite the facts that history have proclaim it to be different, or what white America wants one to believe and the poor old Negro, will believe whatever white America put on the table, without appealing to facts. Being impaired is very essential in the creation of a human machine by being impaired one must be worse than normal to support inferior if, not one must be decreased in strength of the mind since the mind is what make the person.

The reason why' is because one cannot buy quality. Quality has to be an inherited trait as with any self made proposal they must appeal to evil or injury, for a censorship, or banned in others words, and the making of any Negro is no different.

Because of the purpose of the poor old Negro is to serve and perform, and being impaired was essential for success. So in other words, the Negro was a mortar and the owners of the mortar were a success story. And one can very easily say that act was the superior of its kinds and will be very hard to duplicate. One can just say it is one of a kind not to be duplicated again. So if people like Eugene try and duplicate the act by being slick they can only appeal to evil or injury for a repeat performance. And should they get their way it will serve as a censor to the second class citizen in other words, slick Eugene will banned that injured person from their freedom. In other words, one can very safely say that Eugene is a demon and have the same power as any clergyman. Eugene is just like any Santa Claus he holds one back mentally he is not for redemption for his clients the follower. Redemption is to regain, what was lost or to redeem slick Eugene is not trying to rescue the injured the facts will show

Eugene is very selfish and looking out for self. So, in other words, slick Eugene is just a sub- oppressor or another type of oppressor Jesus said it best when he said you either are for me or against me.

Eugene will engaged in a protest of nothing meaning he will not protest, Eugene will go alone with either side of the cause, it's the elements of his principle. In other words, in the Negro phrase he will ride with whoever gives him a ride that's his principle meaning his only principle is self when it come to the Negro. When it comes to white America he's the servant, he knows nothing and will go alone with any cause white America suggests. If he hadn't tried it he is very open minded to engage in any suggestion white America might have 'hey' that was called Uncle Tom back in the day. What one has to understand is that every principle is the representative of self. For instance, one can be all bad and go out and commit a crime and get caught stand up before the judge and cry that shows their real principles and it is self explanatory no wondering here. So, their principle is their real supporting raft just as any rafter supports a roof how strong the rafter is will determined the strength of the roof. Just as a person don't support self, one has nothing imagine what nothing is, slick Eugene supports evil and injustice so if one listen to Eugene they will be control by his thoughts. You are what you think Eugene, is like a preacher who preaches to you about change and in fact they don't have enough faith to change themselves, and when that person don't change that person is control by another force. Eugene is the type of Negro, who will hear about Santa Claus coming down the chimney and when one questioned him about how a fat man comes down a chimney and still be clean. Eugene will still try to explain how it is done in fact he will proclaim he once did it. Eugene will try and frame your thoughts when people reject you they are injuring you because that is the devils main tool it's to reject, one use rejection to slow ones progress.

A dead fish will float down stream a live fish will fight and swim up stream, ones emotions is always connected with their thoughts so therefore, one cannot get their worth from someone else's thought one has to have self control of their emotions to progress. One cannot lay up by the pool and let some -one else think for them that is guaranteed failure, history has plainly demonstrated that. Always look at the fruit of the person who is telling you what to do if, that person is growing a none bearing tree, stay away from that person. Associate with people that are producing a valuable product, demons want to wound your spirit to control you, that will affect your self image and truth is the hardest thing to face. If the demon can't change you they can't hurt you its not about I was its about I am its very easy to go on a diet after a Sunday dinner. Slick Eugene is like a travel agent he's always trying to take you where he has not been. If one can control, what goes into a mind one can control that mind if one can't control what goes into their mind one can't control self. That my friends are the derivable of a good obedient follower they are in a high demand. Eugene is a prime source of how America programmed the poor old Negro with brutality and turned their back on humanity. Dreams must always, out last memory because at the end of life cycle people should say I am not I was. One cannot go to tomorrow while holding on to today the `Negro was programmed with fear that's the very reason why people like Slick Eugene will try and put doubt in ones mind it is to create fear that comes from his genetic base. It's what goes on in one's mind set that determined what goes on in one's mind the mind is still what make the person. You control people by keeping them in in the dark no will, no purpose crush in spirit, those are the kind of people that keeps America going say 'what' well, just look at the penitentiary look at the demand for drugs then, you will see the writer's point. All slick Eugene is trying to do is to be like his original father isn't that his original teacher. Don't sons want to be like fathers of course they do if they are successful? Isn't America successful so why wouldn't anyone want to be like America the writer rest his case? Wrong is the prince of darkness, if one teaches the youth that teaching will impact their life. Then one will program a cycle if people like Eugene

Programmed the youth white America will not have to repair the adults. Eugene condones what white America have to say about darkness, they say it's not a problem with darkness its only a problem when one discover light, and Eugene agrees. Lean not on your understanding lean on me and I will take you there say Eugene and Eugene inherited that from white America. Eugene agrees that when one can't solve a problem you set and do nothing faith, hope, and love was the only thing the Slave had to look forward too.

And love was the strongest of the three so therefore, love was not encouraged love develops unity, unity deliver strength, and strength promotes growth, growth develop value, value promotes self support, and support deliver will. Will guarantees purpose, purpose is one's true character, and character is a supporting component of the mind, and the mind is what make the person so therefore love was out of bounds for the slave. If a person is full of self every time something don't go their way they get mad history has plainly demonstrated that. Pride is very dangerous, pride comes before destruction history has also, demonstrated that all great nations fall nothing last forever not even nothing. Its better be humble than to be humiliated, pride is a feeling of superiority and pride promotes discontent. When a person devalues another person that always comes from a person who has ignorance as their principle, impatience is the fruit of pride, some people you cannot be free around they will upset you or you will upset them that is the fruits of ignorance. One can always tell when a person is full of themselves they will not listen to others because they are to busy, thinking what to say next, history has plainly demonstrated that. They are just full of it whatever you want it to be, whether its ignorance power or both, that person is in need of a complete personal makeover. The preacher will preach to you but will not show you anything. Worry is faith in fear the bible says, fear not, worry paralyzes the mind history has plainly demonstrated that with the poor old Negro. And people like slick Eugene want that cycle to continue because if the mind is paralyze that mind cannot produce.

That person will be carrying the mind around and can't even walk for self they react when someone tells them what, when, and where so that mind is energized by another force enabling that mind to be animated by another spirit. The spirit is the real you and the mind is what make the person. History has plainly demonstrated that with the poor old Negro running around calling themselves black, when in fact many of them are not. But the poor old Negro will embraced, whatever and when ever white America tell them to embrace. That is the same when the master tells his property to jump and the property will ask how high? Do the poor old Negro know they are free all they have to do is unchain themselves from the ignorance. Don't they understand that a dead fish float down stream, when one floats down stream they only stop when they are dammed, then they become stagnated. Don't they understand that live fish swim up stream to fresh water? That's the very reason why rich white masters do not exist in the ghetto, because they are free to choose their decisions, and they do not choose an environment that will dammed their soul because they understand that it is the conditions that dammed the soul. And by association one cannot escape the condition, think my fellow American.

Even though, DNA did not come to light until, the late 80's or the early ninety's but the ones who created the human machine had to have an imagination about DNA and please don't appeal to it just happen. Because every action requires a reaction, just think my brothers and sisters, history has plainly demonstrated that with religion.

No one knew about Religion, until someone turn the religion light on then, it spreaded like a wild fire, in the night by association. But everyday people act like it has existed forever, but according to the Bible and history of this here America they both plainly surrender to truth, and that truth states that it hasn't. Not thinking paralyzes the mind it will put one's mind in a stagnated position, and position remains the greatness spot on the universe. Position has existed since time the same as DNA one can just say it's just hadn't been developed, by developing the mind to an advance position that mind will improve its position so by improving one, then one automatically progresses. One have to understand that DNA is the blue print for future generations otherwise, there would be no advancement for this Universe the ghetto people would be living next door to the Rockyfellows, Kennedy's and etc... In actuality, that doesn't exist because of a blue print, a blue print is a guide to establish or to put in place. So, why would anyone want to establish? The answer is to create a position; history has already demonstrated that with the poor old Negro. The Negro was created to obey and perform, but by association that will change that's the very reason, the Negro is told they are black to keep in place an establish position. And that position is to believe in other rather than self now, does one see how important position is if one's mind is put in a position of thinking that nothing is something, and they convict themselves of that where is the margin for improvement. So, one have to be establish to maintain the original so by being establish, one becomes selfish so by being selfish, there is no need to advance others. Why should one? It can't be for love because love was not including in the original. So why would anyone want to be politically incorrect? Where does benefit lay other than self? So just where is the benefit for the poor old Negro that called themselves black, when in pure facts they are not. Why does one have to curve? When one can be straight and plain, straight and plain derive from absolute and absolute is pure, and pure has not been contaminated. Why contaminate truth? What value does it have for the innocent? The late Mr. Walter Briggs of Beirne Arkansas who had problem reading his name because of only two years of schooling said it best when he said be straight and plain in essence be absolute pure, now on the other side of the spectrum, we have this Harvard graduate who is as white as any white American calling himself black just what message is he sending to this here American children, or future generations he is programming the tomorrow people with not only ignorance but pure falsehood. That has the same effect on one's mind, that Santa Claus has the effect of believing that something is nothing the same effect crack or intoxication have on any human. The bottom line will read to think for self, be straight and plain one cannot serve two master, self is master because you are what you think and you chose what to think from that decision and that decision alone derive one's character and from that character will determine whether one is free or not the writer rests his case thanks Mr. Briggs make peace be upon your soul.

One should be straight and plain, and fight for the resistance of temptation, don't give up the fight. Cause if one's gives up they will become a wonderer, history has plainly demonstrated that the poor old Negro has had to fight for every inch of progress. No fight no progress, it seems to be that way for the Negro, fighting for political correctness should be no exception, the poor old Negro must, turn from addiction. That addiction include the approval of others, the poor old Negro must not cave in to the demands of others. If ones caves in to another force they will be control by that force's spirit, history has plainly demonstrated that. With the light skin Negro declaring themselves black, words are very powerful they are a force by itself they are like a city without boundaries. Without boundaries, one is automatically a pleaser a people pleaser especially. Wisdom is the key to any success, wisdom deliver structure the love of wisdom add kindness and goodness for self. One has to develop fruit, one have to discover their gift and once that gift is discovered one must developed the gift, and that gift is not that of a people pleaser. People pleaser derive from darkness, darkness derive from ignorance, ignorance derive from not knowing, not knowing is the most dangerous position on the universe. Position is the greatness spot on the universe; the poor old Negro was created to be without dignity, since the mind is what make the person the Negro must educate their mind for the mind can educate their emotions. By doing that dignity will arrive but dignity will not derive, from pleasing others, one has to think for self, in order to have a thinking spirit. The mind must educate the spirit. For instance, the very reason why Negroes enjoy lying, drinking, getting high, partying, singing, and going to church they are trying to connect with dignity. Because they don't have the wisdom to know otherwise. Wisdom builds structure for success; The American Negro is across breed the same as a thorough bred horse they both started as crossbreed, but the thoroughbred horse was developed -into a great animal. The same can be said for the American Negro if, only they would think for self and gain wisdom by the knowledge of history. History is absolute, one have to sacrifice to gain love for self, love is sacrifice if one love self they will not degrade self, if one love self, corruption will not destroy one. Falseism, hope, and wrong cannot contaminate one of love with self, the poor old Negro is in a psychological war that derive upon creation and the first causality of any war is truth. Freedom is created by a decision, personal obedience is the only thing that can fix one's life one can over come anything by the choice of freedom that choice is left up to each individual. One has to dwell on success despite the facts that the Negro was programmed to be a failure despite the fact that the Negro was programmed to be content. Ignorance is a very bad burden, and can easily be destroyed just by thinking, but the mind must be programmed to think. It will not derive by hope or chance its has to be established by thinking, it's the law of the mind. One can have a clean heart and a empty hand, the poor old Negro nature depends on their material that is available to them that will determine their mental production.

THE INTENT OF THIS BOOK IS TO INTENSIFY THE AWARENESS OF THE READER

In other words, the intent is to give the reader a broad image of the American Negro.

The intent has already surrendered to truth therefore; the intent will not be a abbreviated portion of truth.

History produces facts, facts signify truth, truth is absolute there are many Negro all over the world. Negroes come in many forms and fashions just to put it mildly, a negro is a crossbreed, a Negro is a cross between any race which is cross with the original man which we believe is black, the one they called the African. Why do we believe the African is the original man? It's very simple my friends, a black can of paint can't be diluted to a darker color, please do not appeal to miracles. Now can we go on and tell what we believe so therefore, any people that signify dark is signified as a Negro.

But the American Negro is a special Negro, created right here in America, by America and for America one cannot escape facts no matter how hard one try.

And please don't appeal to I forgot or I didn't know, the truth will set one free, the poor old American Negro have been trying to free themselves every since their creation. They have appeal to everything except truth, which is the very reason they have not found freedom as we write because they have not surrender to truth. Truth is the root of all good, the American Negro have been programmed to believe that obedience is the root of all good. But, after looking at actuality, actuality broaden one's horizon the American Negro has been obedient every since their creation right here in America. America, America, signify the obedience of the American Negro so if good is the root of obedience of the American Negro so if good is the root of obedience why did the American Negro have to fight to get what they have as we write. For instance, fight to have a God, fight to read and write, fight to have just what every other American have.

But once the fight boils down to actuality it was all about truth if it wasn't for obedience America wouldn't be as we know it as we write.

Obedience paved the way for America when their wasn't any machine to break the rocks to build roads, building like the white house, Harvard University they were all built from obedience. Obedience donated by the American Negro. 'Yes' the writer agree obedience is good but to set and say that obedience is the root of all good is just a myth, history has plainly demonstrated that the poor old Negro has been good so, just why do the innocent poor old Negroes roots reach a dead end at a crack house? When the root system of crack don't start with the Negro and if obedience is good why do crack exist here in America.

If obedience is good, why is the Negro rewarded with something less than good? For instance, being rewarded for something which don't exist or something they already have ignorance. A person innateness will always serve as a base, a base is the beginning or the original so, when a spirit is broken it tries to reconnect that's why all chickens come home to roost.

The writer's father who was an ordained minister in the Church of God in Christ religious sector once said that the poor old Negro was like a wild horse. The writer's father had some experience with wild horses, the writer father; father was credited with owing the last wild horse that was caught in North Texas down on Texas and Oklahoma Boundaries. A white fellow gave the horse to the writer's grandfather why?

According to the white fellow it the horse was just like a ignorant Nigger neither can be modified to exist in a modern world. Just like a snake, when one cut the head off from its body it cannot be reconnected. The white fellow would go on to say if you take the wild horse out of the wild they have no purpose. In essence, what he was saying if you take the Negro away from their master they can't exist so, the poor old Negro will always need a master. In actuality the writer would agree, history has demonstrated that with a light skin

Negro calling themselves black. That prove the fact that the poor old Negro do not want to connect with truth, the Negro just want to be obedient. By being obedient the writer's grandfather took the horse from the white fellow it's seems that the poor old Negro have a trait of taking things from white folks that are worthless and making them of value. For instance back in the days of Slavery, the master children could choose their toys even little Negro children for their toys. Ms Birdie Washington who was the co- author grandmother told a story on how her grandmother was a toy for a little white girl, Ms. Birdie Washington grandmother was a Slave and she would go on to say if the white folks gave you anything you had to take it because the white folks had the power. And the Nigger had nothing that was the last thing the Nigger wanted to do was make the white folks mad. This is the very reason as we write the poor old Negro will call themselves black in fact when they are not. They will consider that as being a gift from their God the white American any gift is better than nothing, any interest shown is better than none. By taking what white America gives one the poor old Negro still hope that someday white America will give them something of value that hope was established from the fruits of Slavery. Ms. Birdie Washington would say you have to keep the white folks happy by them being happy the Negro would automatically be happy, being a toy for master. Every time the little white girl ate Birdie's grandmother would stand behind her, and if Birdie grandmother had made the little white girl happy she would get rewarded. For instance, if the little white girl was eating chicken the little white girl would eat almost all the meat off the bone then the little white girl would give her the unfinished bone. The little white girl would tell her to clean the bone and Birdie grandmother would obey. Now if Birdie grandmother would have upset the little white girl she would eat all the meat off the bone and give the bone to Birdie grandmother and tell her to break the bone but before she broke the bone she would tell her to make a wish. And don't tell any one your wish because if you tell it the wish will not come true, in advance the little white girl had told Birdie grandmother what to wish for the wish was, I wish I had obeyed my mistress if I would have obeyed I would get some meat. Birdie grandmother slept at the foot of her mistress bed on the floor, in other word she was ready 24-7 at thirteen Birdie grandmother gave birth to Birdie mother 'yes' Birdie grandmother, mistress father was the father of Birdie mother, 'yes' Birdie look like a white woman herself. 'Yes' my friends every action stimulate a reaction and any time, someone defy reality all that person is doing is programming a cycle. History has plainly demonstrated that calling themselves black, they are just being very ignorant but obedient. Obedience is the very reason why the writer's grandfather took the horse yet, the grand father would go on to train the horse to be somewhat obedient.

The writer's uncle Jess would take the horse, on weekends and hook it to a wagon and go miles from home to gamble, drink and have a good time. He would get drunk; head the horse in the direction of home pulled the bridle off the horse get in the back of the wagon, and tell the horse to go home. Uncle Jess would put his head under the seat, to protect him from the elements, if it was winter time this uncle Jess would wrap up in a quilt. The writer's father would say, on Monday morning Jess would be all wrap up asleep just as if he was in a sleeper in a 18 wheeler. When someone woke him up he would get up and drink a cup of coffee and go into the field to do his daily work. Now on the other side of the spectrum, if the horse decided to go back to the wild in his mental capacity when this uncle Jess would tie the horse up, if the horse was in his wild capacity the horse would just pulled a loose and go home the writer's father would say if that happen the post or whatever he was tied to would still be tied to the horse but no Jess in the wagon so, the writer father would go on and say, that was one crazy horse but he wasn't that crazy, because he returned to the base of operation home. The father would go on to say just like any chicken they always come home to roost and the poor old Negro is no exception. So in essence, by breaking one spirit and programming one with the materials the programmer want, the programmer will have an endowment for the future. The future will read there are three groups of Negroes basically with more than one million incarcerated, the rest or either in the hood or being very obedient and stand behind master waiting on their handout the message haven't change only the events have changed .

The intent of this book is to bring truth to the forefront, just as the Africans was rounded up in Africa, wild and naked, running wild, and free. The average American Negro do not understand or care what freedom means Negroes have a problem with freedom. Freedom require decisions, Negroes will make rational or irrational decisions.

If that decision do not benefit the Negro and the Negro future generation how can that decision be rational, one must remember the seed is in the deed. Where does the benefit lies in being incarcerated? How can ones' generation benefit by being incarcerated?

How can one benefit by lying to self? Don't one understand they are `programming a cycle all one has to do is think and that is the very intent of this book is to get one to think. By thinking, thinking will get one to change one's horizon. One's thinking is no different from any one else, one's thinking is the same as one's gift everything has a beginning a developing stage, a conclusion thinking is no different. One has to developed their thinking in order for it to perpetuate the body has a peak period, for only a short period of its existence. Then, it begins a process of deteriorating thinking is no different that's the law of nature. There is only two sides to everything, either you are or you are not, either you are dead or alive, day or night, right or wrong, advancing or decreasing nothing stays the same. That's seems to be the law of nature, the poor old Negro tries too defy that law. It seems that the law of mathematics is the only pure science just as truth is the only pure facts and to my Negro friends please do not appeal to Mr. Charlie. The intent of this book is to educate

Just because one is educated that don't indicate that they are a captain know it all, they only know what they have learned meaning the boundaries of their mental acceptance. This book is about choice, this book is about freedom, this book is not about hatred, this book is not how bad the ingredient of America have served the poor old Negro. This book is about choice and decisions that was made to create this American typical Negro, it's about the freedom that was given to the American Negro. It's about the pure facts on how the American Negro, had to fight for freedom, the predicament the Negro had to choose from, and the results of that choice. What was that predicament? Was it a blessing or a curse? Each American Negro decides that choice now that's a` decision, one can believe what they want but the facts remains the same. The intent is not to persuade, the intent is to put truth on the table, history is pure, and history will be ones best teacher if history is given a chance DNA is the blue print for each individual, future generations and each generation will have a choice, by setting and doing nothing is a choice. By following someone else' idea logics that's a choice, by thinking for self, and creating a imagination and that's a choice. Since everything has to start with an imagination, any imagination will shed light on darkness wrong is the prince of darkness. So why would anyone want to be a mortar for wrong, this goes back to the ignorance of not knowing their purpose in other words, their idea logic's is established from their original of their innateness. By the time, this book is printed America will have another cross breed president; history has provided us with that information. The cross breed is a cross between a African and a so- called white American it seems that the poor old Negro is literally taken this as a first. What are we going to do with Abe Lincoln and president Obama resemblance?

Why don't the poor old Negro look at facts? President Obama is not black, nor is he an American Negro. The only thing Mr. Obama and the American Negro have in common is their originality, that's what science would say. Mr. Obama father did not come to this America in chains, Mr. Obama was not raised in the ghetto, and Mr. Obama was not raised by the American Negro. One simply can't compare something that existed for over 400 years, to something that don't exist at all. The intent of this book is for one, one meaning people to let truth set them free, people meaning all people, the writer hope all people will enjoy this book.

CHAPTER I

WHO AM I
THE WRITER IS THE PRIDE GREAT GRANDSON
OF EBENEZER LAFAYETTE DOHONEY:

JUST WHO AM I, THAT'S the big question that lies before every American Negro who am I, that's the age long question to every American Negro. In actuality the poor old American Negro don't know, they only know they exists. The American Negro can be compared to a piece of meat or waste when one goes to the market for meat they buy it or jack it then, consume the meat. Then the meat serves its purpose then the human discord the meat as waste, most humans don't have the slightest clue on where on where or how the meat derived. All they know they are consuming what is none as meat but the true identity is not known, so, we take it as we find it, and assume it has existed forever. The same as when the meat leaves the human body, most human don't have the slightest idea where the waste goes. As Coach DeHorney would say out of sight out of mind, or as Ervin Gardner would say better out than in. The writer remembers when raw sewage was dumped right into the Colorado River in Yuma Arizona.

And guess what was consuming the human waste 'yep' you are right fish, the writer remembers how people would boast on how big the fish were in the Colorado River. Most people didn't have the slightest idea on what the fish were eating; they were eating human waste that existed until the late sixty's when the City built a treatment plant. Now the sewage is used as fertilize not knowing is the most dangerous spot on the Universe.

Man the writer have hauled many a load of treated waste and dumped into the fields to feed many a plants.

The American Negro is no different by the existence of not knowing, the poor old Negro seems by not knowing they do care to no and from how the poor old Negro sees' it one can't miss what they don't have but, as the late Guthrie Briggs would say I don't care don't have a home. By that parable, that is the very reason why the American Negro is in a position of wondering, and position is the greatest spot on the Universe.

Readers get use to this phrase it will be use many times in this book, that's the very reason the writer called his long time acquaintance Alexander Dees down in Yuma Arizona because he was in position to help the writer with this book. Just who is this Alexander Dees? First and foremost, he is an American Negro furthermore, he is a professional cattle rancher and a Brangus breeder and is recognize by the Brangus association as one of America's top breeders. So whose' in a better position to explain about the genetics than Mr. Dees. To abbreviate his resume, he has over forty years as a Brangus breeder and over forty years as a consultant and a national official judge of cattle, so from the light of experience one should always, go to the best for the best enlighten. The bible says, love is more valuable than gold that's one of many principles of the bible and all principles will surrender to reality.

When the writer called Mr. Dees. The writer the writer asked are you busy? I need about ten minutes of your time, Mr. Dees replied rapidly, I am always busy, but if you thought enough of my advice I can't help but give you some of my time. That was a response of innate love that's a quality one can't buy, it has to come from above. That character is an inherited trait it derives form one's genetic pool. Mr. Dees didn't have the Audrey Brown Rayford of Fannin County mental component. The writer have lived long enough to have the experience to recognize quality that derive from the soul. The soul derive from one's inherited trait, one's soul cannot be transformed that's pure and simple as with any truth. Truth derive from will, will derive from purpose, and purpose is a true quality that derive from one's soul.

When one's soul derives from their genetic pool, it has a purpose it was breaded for a purpose whether or not it's a Negro or a show animal. Whether it's a rich person or a poor person will depend on the will, the will, will depend on the genetics the genetics will depend on the quality from which the soul derives. It will be innate by nature and please don't appeal to miracles they are not part of the mix. One's soul will be that of three types of quality improve, consistence, or decrease species.

So in essence, what the writer is saying the mind is what make the person, if one breed with the same type mind the mind will be consistent. Now if the lower mind breed with a higher type mind the chances are very good of getting an improve variety it's a fifty-- fifty chance. Or can one just say it's only a possibility at best, but for sure we know it can decrease and please don't be like the poor old Negro go out and breed with what-ever and pray and hope for a miracle.

Writer what are you talking about? Yes it's time to get to the point, the writer is talking about the first load of Africans that came to this here America they were not the best of what's what in Africa they were the lower caliber or the lower type the same one we see on television as we write that's in need of help. The less desirable, that was the nomads of yesterday no doctors, no lawyers, no kings, no queens just humans in need of transformation of the mind. Since the mind is what make the person, now these are the people which were brought to this here America on that first ship good Jesus in 1552, when America seen these people wouldn't serve their purpose the Americans had to make a decision on what to do.

So the decision was to breed the African with the whites to get a new variety, from that mix of species they came up with a new species. And it perpetuated to what it is as we know it as we write the American Negro had arrived. A new type species for America only which had Africa's finger print on it. So in other words the poor old Negro was created to solve a problem, America was going to take the red man land so they needed farm workers. By creating the American Negro that solve a problem for America and created a whole new and different variety of species including the writer.

The writer is no different than any other American Negro, he is a mix variety that was created right here in this America the writer have heard studies that the poor old American Negro is 85% mix but the writer will argue with that stats. The writer will go as far to say that all Negroes are mixed. History say that the last ship came to this here America in 1858, so from that point to the existing time as we write that's 15% still stands. What kind of stuff were those people smoking? Almost impossible, a snowball would stand a chance surviving in hell, than a pure African surviving from Slavery. When the writer was growing up the writer would ask his father, father who am I? Father would reply you are Jun Dehorney. Father where did I come from? Father would reply you came from Africa, the writer would reply why am I light skin? Father would reply my father was half white. The writer asked what was my grandfather daddy name? The writer father would say I don't know I only seen him three times, I didn't asked his name. Why didn't you asked his name father? Father would say I was young. So tell me how I came from Africa? Well son you didn't come from Africa. How do that work father? Did my mother find me under a tree like the cows find their calf under a tree? By that time, the writer's mother would hear the conversation and would say boy you go and play you are getting to Manish. The writer was fourteen when he really found out were a calf came from about the same time, the writer's father started teaching him about what the poor old Negro would describe as birds and bees. The Negroes from this community was just ignorant what other way can you describe it. They tried to protect and preserve the Negro ignorance, as the poor old Negro would describe it they would sweep it under the rug for safe keeping. The writer's father would tell the writer if you don't know it can't hurt you, you can't miss what you don't have all the writer knew at that point was his great grand father was a white man from Paris Texas. And his great grand mother was an ex- Slave and the writer and the writer's grandfather was born sometime before the civil war. They all came from Kentucky in the same covered wagon in 1859, to Paris Texas. The writer's father would boast about how his father knew Jesse and Frank James, Cold Younger, Bloody Bill Anderson, and William Quantrill.

The writer often wondered about all of that with the help of his late uncle Charley DeHorney he made it plain and simple the whole story the truth, the year was 1978.

The writer's father was as white as any white American and he had real thin blond hair, even had the blue eyes, He was lighter than the average so - called white American but the writer's father classified himself as a colored man and was proud of it. The writer asked his father many times why you didn't go for white father. The father replied the bible tell us to obey those who have rule over you the writer would reply, don't know one know but you. The writer father would say the Lord knows that I am colored and that's what matters.

One will always display their intellect, just like one can't swim where there is no water that's the typical American Negro. The writer's father displayed the same genetics that everyone display they all displays what they have available to them. The writer's father was a victim of the fruits of slavery; it was the condition of ignorance that dammed his soul. It was the condition that dammed his mental machine not to asked names and not to seek knowledge that's only a small fraction of the whole scenario.

The writer's father mother was a full blood Choctaw Indian this is a book by itself, and we will spare you the reader the details and get to the point the writer want to make.

In 2007, the writer called his late sister Emma Jean Sweet -- DeHorney and asked her did she know the writer's grandmother mother's name? And Jean replied no I don't know but she always wore an apron and smoked a pipe. As Bubba would say one can't swim where there is no water. In 1999, the writer's cousin Lucille DeHoney -Harvey came to Arizona to visit her son and she called the writer. She asked if the writer could come and pick her up because she wanted to talk. She talked about the DeHoney's history since her father was a older brother to the writer's father which meant he knew more specifics about the family. And that was the switch that turn the knowledge of light on that really put the machine in motion. It was just a small missing link, she said she was trying to find out our great -grandfather name but she didn't know how. Her father name was Luss DeHoney as you can plainly see that the spelling of the names are different. The information Luss DeHoney left behind was that he didn't know his grandfather name but he did know he was from Paris Texas. He had wrote some books, and was a State Senator who's name was on the original hand book of Texas.

Which means he helped wrote the original state constitution of Texas that govern Texas as we write. That was very simple, how many state senators from Paris Texas held that honor? Only one, Lucille would go on to say she tried many times to get help from her children but to no avail. The writer can relate to that experience, upon receiving that precious information the writer would like to think of it as a gift from above. He immediately, called his son who lives in Texas and was a history teacher with two degrees, and asked could he check into this hand book of Texas. The son never got back with the writer, after about a week the writer called his son and the son said the hand book got lost over the Years and the writer will quote him "dad you know they didn't have copy machines in 1876, and there is no way to find out what names are on the original state constitution". The poor old Negro hold their hands to tight and they really don't understand that nothing is in them. Just think if the chicken was like the Negro we would not be eating chicken eggs, and chickens. Nobody has to tell the chicken to come out of the egg the chicken want too, the poor old Negro have to be spoon fed and even force fed that's the typical American Negro.

After that incident, after searching documents, several documents it became very simple thanks to the laws of mathematics, mathematics is the only pure science.

The poor old American Negro that was created right here in America, for America, and by America, meaning they where born right here in America to be an endowment for future America. We know you the reader have heard the slogan made in America so, history has demonstrated that the poor old Negro was not only made in America they were made for America and exclusively to be used by America only. That was fine and dandy for the creators, but it was a mental disaster for the poor old Negro, the Negro is still suffering the effects of that creation as we write. So the Negro need to go through a transformation to understand self without the aid of transformation the Negro will be lodged between no where and nothing. Can one imagine nothing? So could that be the main reason that the Negro owned more land in 1900 than as we write? Is that proof enough that the Negroes genetics in on the decline? One can surely wonder since the Negro is a wonderer by nature. That is one of many inherited traits it runs neck and neck in ignorance, ignorance leads by a head the Negro have receive no help for that problem no studies or research on the Negroes problem that's out of bound at the research center. As the Christian religion said back in the day those Negro problems, are those Negroes problems, God sent them for our endowment just think America the Negro problem is America's problem. Just think of that the next time you go hug your grand children and see if they have the man's finger prints on them. And if they don't they will sooner or later all chickens come home to roost, if one don't go through a transformation they will never understand the original problem. Especially, the poor old American Negro 'hey' it derive right there in Africa as the wild Africans was rounded up like any stray cattle and driven to a holding pen called fort Jesus. 'Hey' don't get mad at the writer get mad at history and come together to help this America to be a better America don't get mad at truth, the truth will set one free.

The poor old Negro had been at a psychological war with self every since their creation just to please their creator, and the first casualty of any war is truth. The rest of America have been at a psychological war with themselves to hide the truth in other words, they are in a delusional state of mind. And all parties must be transformed as one in order to help mankind until, that comes together hate and discontent will remain and there will be no Peace. Fort Jesus, was used as a holding pen for the Slave ships to transport the African to American the Africans was packed on the ships like sardines in a can. The condition was like any cattle truck of today where they are packed so tight for there will be no movement. Because they do not want the cows too fall if they fall the cargo becomes damaged or any movement will cause the truck or ship to tilt sturdy is the aim. Federal guidelines require the cattle trucks to inspect their cargo, every two hour to rest the cows.

Their was no guidelines for the Africans only the strong survived but on a cattle truck there is to be no inhumane treatment that's the law of this here America. You never see a cattle truck pulled over for speeding even when the speed limit were 55ph never a bad looking cattle truck its always big cars pulling cattle trailers. And no Negroes driving those big cars what's up with that? The writer heard the Negro was not ready for prime time. There was no inhumane concern for the Africans not even the Christian religion was concerned they were chained hand and feet, they stayed in place standing -up sometime two weeks at a time. They were naked and relieved themselves like any cattle, on a cattle truck they were programming the future American Negro to be 50% of the creation to come.

Some of the same Africans that were rounded up and was at fort Jesus escape the trip to America because of the cut -off in 1858, they were all united by blood, or environment.

So, they continued in their ways of wondering, their past became their future so one can very well say, that the one that was left behind and the ones made it to America was one of the same species.

As the writer's great grandfather said they were of the lower type animal, the writer great-grand father who was Ebenezer Lafayette Dohoney who was a former Slave owner, who had a family tradition that started in 1723, they were known for breeding humans for Slaves just as Alexander Dees is for breeding Brangus cattle They had the same type resume, by that pedigree no one knows the Negro better than the master. E.L. Dohoney would go on to say, that the lower type animal which was the African was the first creation of the earth, the second creation of man was the white race who was ordained by God to rule the earth.

'Yes' this E.L. Dohoney was a very religious man, his family was so religious if was as though they were God sent yes he have the backing of the holy bible about the two creation it will be explain in the last chapter of this book. E.L. Dohoney would go on to say that the same type species that was bought to this here America was refined by creation to be a new variety known as the American Negro. No doubt those same type species, which was brought to America, would someday later return as a new type species to help their former family their brothers and sisters of Africa. They would return and help those species be a better species, and as we write that is exactly what happening. E.L. Dohoney wrote that in the 1800.'S

Now that is the writer bloodline, the writer has 1/8 of that man's blood running through his veins. And the writer certainly agrees with the late Texas historian Clarence Wharton when he said that Ebenezer Lafayette Dohoney was an advance thinker, a man born Years before his time. And would say the lawyer, and politician, was one of the 50 men who had exerted the greatness influence in Texas.

The editor of the handbook of Texas thought enough of Ebenezer Lafayette Dohoney important enough to be included in part of Texas history to include almost a half- page of his resume. His resume includes he became the father of the homestead act of 1871.

The writer would agree with the poor old Negro Texas is a big old State since genetics determined ones soul and the soul determine the mind, and the mind is what make the person. The person has no choice of where the soul derives from.

E. L. Dohoney wrote that there has never been a greater crime than that what was Impose on the Negro, but on the other side of the dark deep blue waters of chance the poor old Negro is one thousand percent better off with their atrocity they went through than if they had stayed in their native land. The writer's son coach J.R. would agree with that with the atrocity he went through growing up as a child he had to be tied up and drug to the scene of enlighten. Despite his rejection and criticism by others by the fruits of obedience he has two degrees but his criticizers hasn't any they are just the typical American Negro which is matter taking up space. As the writer's great -grand father E.L. Dohoney would say, the typical American Negro is just like a rocking chair they work, get high, and lie but they stay in the same position, and position is the greatness spot on the Universe. But Bubba would say the typical American Negro still thinks that by working that will guarantee them success, in actuality that's only a myth.

The cow above is just the typical American Negroes cow in fact it can be compared to the poor old Negro. It has no none pedigree, it is what the poor old Negro would call a sooner, sooner one thing as another just like the Negro whatever one calls it it's okay. This is how the Negroes animals looked in Ravenna Texas when the writer was growing up there, and this is not the writer's cow.

As you the reader can see the cow has a yolk around it's neck, the purpose of the yolk is to contain the cow the same with the typical Negro. All American Negroes have that yolk although it is invisible the power of the yolk still exists. Or can we just say the Negro yolk is around their mind the mind that derive from their genetics. Since genetics powers the mind one must not forget the mind is what make the person.

The picture above is a Holstein cow, its breed is recognize by through out the Universe. Unlike the poor old Negro the Holstein pedigree can go to the beginning of the breed its genetics has joy, peace, and happiness which derives from a care giver.

It's very proud of its heritage unlike the American Negro who doesn't know the existence of yesterday because the master programs the American Negro with fear and ignorance. Telling the Negro that one can't go to the future by holding on to the present but on the other side of the spectrum, if it was not for yesterday there wouldn't be any Holstein cow today.

The same with the poor old Negro today is yesterday's history, one cannot and must not forget that the mind is what makes the person and that mind derive from one's genetic pool.

CHAPTER II

THE BEGININNG:

JUST LIKE ANY SUPER MIND one has to have an imagination of what one create without thinking, one cannot do that one has to have imagination about creating the American Negro you are what you think. Every thing comes by the way of thinking, a way of thinking or non- thinking in other words, what the writer is trying to say is that everything which is successful it just don't happen, you have to have an imagination of what one wants. And creating the American Negro is no different first one must think from thinking a choice is born, from that choice a decision is made, and from that decision a habit is formed. Now from that habit a character derives, from character promotes growth from growth an image is developed.

And from that development evolution begin nothing will ever be the same from that day forward.

The poor old American Negro didn't just drop out of the sky it was a plan, an execution by the American whites. No matter how hard one tries one cannot escape their past or from their reflection. Not the Negro or the American whites the Negro was created to be a mortar for America and for that to perpetuate the Negro would become an endowment for America which we so love as we speak just as one keep bad company, all bad company does is corrupt one. The same applies to the poor old Negro the one that was created for the endowment for the American whites. It was all good for the American whites but is corrupt for the poor old Negro as we will find out as we continue this book about how the American Negro was created not only to be an endowment but a mortar for America's whites. We will say America because the America's whites who owns America we are talking about the rich whites, not the America's poor but the poor ones does have an opportunity the one that was denied the poor old Negro all one need to be successful in this here America is to have an opportunity. By being denied and rejected one wasn't included in the dream for America the only thing the American Negro had or could hope for was a painful nightmare.

Just as the American whites had a saying to focus on what you have and not what you don't have they implanted or program that into the American Negro to focus on what they had and not on what they didn't have that would go to explain why the American Negro hopes there is no value in hope. Hope only serve as what one want so one can very well say that is why the Negro hopes so much because one should focus on positive thinking only, position thinking during Slavery was hoping that some day All of this would all be over. That's the only positive thing the Negro had to look forward too and one could very well say that is why the American Negro put so much emphasis on hope as we write. They were developing a root system a way of thinking which in reality it really is dysfunctional.

Before we move on let the writer explain what a Negro is many people don't understand what a Negro is because America want to escape their past that's why America teaches the Negro to go from this day forward and not to include the past, one cannot escape their past no matter how hard one tries. Well American derives from all over the world if one just think who ever was a Slave owner 99.9% of them had something to do with the creation of the American Negro. America want one to think that the American Negro solely arrive from Africa 'yes' the African was rounded up in Africa because Africa wanted to get rid of what we called the today as homeless people, sorry people which at that time they were called nomads they was just running wild in Africa and they had created their own environment. They put them out of villages and cities and so forth, in Africa because they were what they called undesirable them they starter breeding among themselves and it just perpetuated the undesirable problem.

The following began around 10,000 B.C. hunters/ gathers Nomads Neolithic {originating in the Middle East}. They were the first farmers.

Mesolithic {originating in {Egypt} began in the middle stone age {8,000B.C.}

They followed mammoths and other large mammals, making huts from skins. Mesolithic Nomads migrating to Eastern Europe began farming around 5,000B.C.

So, America needed workers to work their farms that they had taken away from the red man then, by thinking the Africa pops -up in their mental computer. They went over to Africa and made a deal with Africa and once they brought them over the American whites began impregnating the women immediately on the first ship. And that was the creation of a lot of problems including venereal disease which they the American whites already had from mixing and mingling with their own kind before they mixed with the Africans.

When the Africans arrived in American the African wouldn't work just imagine how you go out and try to tame a wild animal? One just can't talk to that animal one has to have some type of way of communicating with the animal and America was still in there primitive state of mind. The only thing they could come up with was to instill fear into the poor African, and from that fear that created the Negro we know today fear done that not love fear.

So why in ones wildest dream do you the reader think that on the way to America with the first load of Africans and one of the American that went in there, and who had help captured the Africans and she was tied up with chains, her hands were chained, her feet was chained, and they had no were to use the bathroom and they just stood up, and relieve themselves on themselves. They were naked they wasn't given any clothes they just came over as they were they strip them of everything their language, their god, now do you think that African woman was just ignorant but they were wild now just let the white American male come and take her by the hand come on honey lets have sex and she complied, the writer think not. The writer has caught lots and lots of wild animals and never once have they acted like they were tamed. Just like any wild horse who is running in the wild you have to get into the psyche of that horse before that horse would obey no doubt the African were no different so, what they done was raped the African women the men were out there it took them about three months to get from African to America and what were the men doing for sex? Other than having sex with each other no shower facilities they were nasty and then immediately they started what would become the norm for white America males having sex and spreading diseases not with only the African females but the African males. History has plainly demonstrated that. The writer suffer blindness now from the fruits of slavery.

We the writer have experience in this here because experience is ones best teacher history don't lie. One can believe what they want but the facts remain the same. So by breeding with the wild Africans upon arrival there were many Africans women pregnant and once the babies were born and you know how America loves to experiment love to take down stats that's America's way. It all started in America on that slave ship by experimenting and taking notes and comparing the African with the newborn malotto is what they called is a cross between a purebred African and whatever the whites called themselves. From that genetic pool that's what makes the American Negro multi in other words, one can just say that the American Negro is a little bit of this and a little bit of that .That is the Way the poor old Negro describes it. The same would be said about the American Negroes split personality it derives from their genetic pool. After the mulatoo was created white American breeding back into the mulattoo and created the making of a real pretty yellow Negro. The Africans have laid claim that they are the original man the black man and when they germinate they put their brand on all future generations so one can very well say that any dark skin person in the world their roots derives from the black man the African the original man. Hello America how are you? Let us the writer and the reader create an imagination for ourselves let suppose we were wild humans running free not worrying about nothing but just how we were going to survive. In the first place we would already be dysfunctional by being out of a well cared for community. Now if we were put out of that community for whatever reason we would immediately go into shock and once the shock period is over we would be permanently damage. We would never be the same just like any plant you go set out a plant any living plant if the plant is disruptive it would be damage somewhere sometimes they survive sometimes they don't but immediately the process of evolution begins. The wild African is no different that's one shock right there and they will be permanently damage and it become part of the root system or genetic pool. The mental mind, now suppose you are captive well there is another mental shock now supposing you are raped if you are a woman it's another mental shock if you are taken to a foreign land that's another mental shock. Then, you are incarcerated that's another mental shock and you have no chance of escaping what would be your alternative can you set up and try to adjust or would you just dream probably the writer would like to think it would be a combination of both. Now what would that produce? Now you have been portrayed by your guards, by your masters, then if you was a man you would be degraded now if you was a woman the master would want you to be submissive. How would that impair your mind? You think about that you the reader well after one think about it for a while one would probably think as the writer does ones human rights had been violated. Then just like any woman when she is been raped her rights are being violated the same goes with the mind when you captured a person and taken them prisoner you mentally have been raped meaning your mind have been damage. Just like a homeless person their mind have been damage that's the reason they are homeless they are mentally imbalance so automatically right there one becomes dysfunctional you cannot function as the person who is raping you. Because there are two different identities at work in other words, there are two different thoughts processes working at the same time by two different individuals... But each one has something in common how to oppress the other one thought, the winner will be the survival of the strongest well, that remind me of a story that is very much real. The writer's father was a jack of all trades and the only thing he mastered was being obedient so this rich white man own this big farm at one time it was the home for slaves my father worked on that plantation and the white man had a mule that went way back the mule was about 25 years old. The mule was wild never had been tamed the mule had never been trained for any purpose he just roamed free as the wind he was a very large grey mule for whatever reason my father tried to tame the mule he obtained the mule and brought him to our place and tried to train him to be a work mule But, the mule would be just like the wild Africans he would have a mind of his own so the writer's dad worked with the mule for a couple of weeks and he was working very gentle with the mule and he decided to hook him up to a plough by himself he the writer's father thought it was time. When he hook the mule up to the plough they took off and they went about 100 yards it was all good and beautiful and he the writer father pick the plough up out of the ground to returned to where they started the mule's mind return back to the wild and the mule took off running it was all the writer dad could do was to get the mule stopped after he had ran into the fence. Because he didn't want any harm to come to the mule. The mule was running while dragging the plough the writer dad was trying to hold the mule can you the reader imagine, something like 1600 hundred pound mule against a one hundred and sixty pound man needless, to say the writer's dad didn't have a chance. The mule had not developed doubt because the mule had not been program with fear. When the stimulus was concluded the writers father brought the mule into a holding pen and got a whip and started whipping the mule to try to install fear into the mule but to no avail. To say the least one can believe whatever they want but the fact will remain the same it will be the same as one who is trying to run from their shadow. Wildness speak for itself the African was no different you go back to the law of nature if one does the same thing as another wouldn't you the reader agree that one would get the same result that's the law of nature. Just like you would see any homeless person staying on the street as the nomads were would you the reader classify that person as mentally challenge. They would already be dysfunctional the wild African was no different they came over as dysfunctional now wouldn't you the reader agree that is someone just like for instance, this African was standing up feet chained to the side or to the bottom of the deck and her arms was chained to the side or top and she was naked and did not have no where for her private moments. And here some man just because he wanted to have sex with her he would unlatch her and take her and rape her would you the reader describe him as a normal human being. Or would you describe that person as dysfunctional? Yes you are ever so right now those two get together and make a baby now how could the baby come here thinking any other way except abnormal. The only thing that could be in that baby genetics is that of a dysfunctional bloodline That my friend was the creation of the American negro as we know them as we write. As with any baby the baby will have to be programmed now you the reader think in your wildest mind that the baby would come here speaking English, or its native tongue. A Spanish baby come her speaking Spanish because the mothers program the baby to speak Spanish a English speaking mother would program her baby the only thing she know which would be English. A Navajo that spoke nothing but Navajo would program her baby to speak Navajo that's the law of nature. So how can this baby the cross between the African and the white be born with any other substance outside the two genetic pool that come together to make a baby. At this point a question has arrive who taught the baby English since the mother did not speak English remember the wild African was strip of everything but their ignorant and blackness. That was the only thing they could bring to this here America they were promise a new identity that started with their language English would be the norm. The writer's great-grand –father wrote that the first generation of mulatto/a was raised by white America the babies were taken away from their mothers the wild Africans. In other words, what the writer is saying the original mulatto/a babies were taken away from their mothers and programmed by the American whites. So, one can safely say that the original mulatto/a serve as a teacher to help program the future generation and new arrivals of the Africans. From that original generation it served as a base for the future for the American Negro as we know them as we write English was implanted in all Negroes mind since the mind is what make the person. So in order to have a very successful Negro slave the Negro mind had to be impaired otherwise the Negro would not work mentally or physically for this here America. It would be just like that mule the writer father tried to break, impairment was a must for America to be successful as we know it as we write, so by being impaired in the mind set that automatically makes one dysfunctional. So the super minded American who came up with the idea of enslaving Negroes and by breeding the Negro by creating his own race in other words, one can say he just invented his own human. So by inventing his own human to serve America's purpose you have to have a dysfunctional mind to start with and by impairing being impaired they wanted the American Negro to be worse off as they could. In other words, instead of improving the situation they wanted to worsen the situation, the worse the situation was, the better it would be for America. America was growing and America was planting a seed one can very well say that America planted the seed of ignorance in the American Negro otherwise; America's program would not be successful. Because the mind is what make the person the intellect takes advantage of the simple when a person is in darkness they act like their in darkness. They don't act like they are in the light if you do not believe the writer just blindfold yourself and see how you react to the situation so, you don't act like you can see. Just like an impaired person they don't act like they know what they are doing they only do what they are told to do or what they are program to do. All one has to do is think so just like the making of any machine the machine requires a maker and the machine will be made to suit the maker. And the mechanics of the machine will be made to serve the maker since the mind is what make the person. And if you want that person to work for you one will have to decrease their ability to think one will have to put something else on their mind to decrease their strength. If you find a baby one should program it on how they want it to be if you want the baby to be smart you will teach him how to be smart. Teach him to read by with holding information from the mind you decreases his ability to think all one has to do is think. So what the writer is saying when a baby is born by law of inheritance they are going to have traits of both sides of the party. Meaning, his mother and father now the negro who had white fathers one has to take and decrease that baby inequality because otherwise, that baby will pick up traits from their father the white man now remember the white man is the one who is thinking how to have a good servant they don't want their babies thinking {the negro baby} they were born to be discriminated against. They had to decrease their quality because the baby is going to have traits like both parties that's the law of inheritance. Now just from the laws of inheritance that baby is going to have some character, the traits of character from their father that is the law of inheritance. By inherited the law of nature one can not go out and buy quality it has to be inherited so if one have inherited certain traits of quality if one want a good slave what one will have to do is decrease that give them something other than what they were born with. One cannot run from their reflection the same as one cannot run from their shadow one can turn from their shadow but the reflection will always remain. Now you the reader just think with the writer for a moment you can take a Holstein cow which is black and white you continue to breed that cow back with the same kind don't one know you will get the same results. And the quality will remain the same and if you want to worsen that you have to decrease the strength that lies within the original. The making of the American Negro is no different from the making of any machine all machines require a machine maker. There is no different with the making of the American Negro "hello" America how are you? I am your native son the writer. Just like any genetic pool the writer was told one can take ones genetics and put them in a soda water bottle and shake them up. Then pour the amount that one need to form a human then therefore what the writer is saying if you take good genetics, bad genetics, smart genetics, and dumb genetics and when you mix them up all will not come back as one want it will be something that comes in there that is not wanted. Just like when one take the super mind the white American and breed those with the wild African one will get traits from both parties. So therefore that goes to explain why white America taught the American negro to be against the American negro to nullify any chance of a duplicate of themselves the American whites the maker.

In other words, the American whites did not want any chance of the role to be reversed. One must understand that a chain is only as strong as its weakest link the American Negro is no different. The super mind understood that all so well one can very well say the whites American was supplied by the American Negro a comfort zone. The poor old Negro sweated for cried for, and bled for the American whites that can very well help explain why the American whites do not suffer from hypertension. Because the poor old negro have been program to worry for white America that enable white America to have and enjoy the comfort of a comfort zone. The poor old Negro did everything possible to keep white American in their comfort zone if it meant lying, if it meant stealing, if it meant doing without, if it meant suffering the poor old Negro carry out the wishes of white America. One can very well say that the poor old negro at one period of time thought that the wishes of white American were meant as a demand for the poor old negroes white American wanted to stay in the comfort zone and the poor old negro was program to give white American what they wanted as the poor old negro would say believe you me they did. That fate still assist as we write otherwise, why you the reader think the American penitentiaries are full of Negroes the American whites didn't create the American Negro to be free. The American Negro was created to serve and perform history have plainly demonstrated that and the present hasn't change that is the conclusion that time don't change only the events of time change. One can very well say that the writer father had a valid point when he said that if one mistreats the womb they mistreat themselves the Negro is the womb. The negro didn't ask to come here we all know so well that the American whites were the ones that created the American negro history has plainly demonstrated that. With the yellow skin of the Negro, The American Negro is not only a reflection of the past but also a reflection of white America history has proven one cannot run from their shadow. America will not exist as we know it today without the America Negro. History has already demonstrated that with the decline of Mississippi every disaster start somewhere every end begins somewhere. One has to surrender to truth one cannot lie forever and exist in falsehood the Santa Clause effect don't last forever. One can very well say that the Negro creator the American whites had to have a spilt personality one for his Negro children and one for his so called white children. One would be precious and all good the other would be used for an endowment one can plainly see that the creation of the Negro could not escape the dual purpose of the mind dual meaning split personality because there is only one love. Love cannot be split into two parts one will love one and hate the other.

History has plainly demonstrated that with the creation of the American Negro. History has plainly demonstrated which one the creator hates and which one the creator love the creator has plainly demonstrated that they couldn't or wouldn't love both sets of children. The creator of the American Negro had two sets of children and two sets of rules one for his so called whites and the other for his Negro children. For instance one stayed in the big house the mansion walked on marble floors sleep on cotton mattress and was taught to read and write. And on the other side of the spectrum, they lived in a one room shack walk on dirt floors they slept on straw beds and were denied the opportunity to read and write and one was taught a religion and the other was denied the right to a religion for over 200 years but both children had the same amount of genetics from their father the same man the white American. One was looked upon as a trophy, the other one was looked upon as an investment or an endowment for the future generations to come. One can very well say that the white American blessed his so- called white children and bestowed a curse upon his Negro children to last for ever and forever is a long time. The curse still exists as we write today that's over 400 years my friends.

A picture is worth a thousand words, the picture above shows Fred Engle of Chandler going up for a lay- up. He stole the ball from Yuma high guards and he had to have an imagination of what he wanted before he stole the ball.

The same principle the founding fathers, of America had before going to Africa to bring the Africans to America. They had to have an imagination of what they wanted in other words; they had to have a purpose as did Engle. Otherwise, he would have set and did nothing that was his choice, choice derives from the mind. But often the imagination comes from others, to the left is the writer notice how fat the writer was {not} notice the muscle tone and the depth of the writers' legs but he was classified as been fat by his brother Thurman. Ignorance derives from not knowing, and words are very powerful and words can destroy one's mind, words can create fear or success words are the structure to a believer. In other words, words are the principles of nothing to the prince of darkness.

Behind the writer in the picture is Mike Bundy and also, Mike Harris the writer illustrated the picture to show the power of position. But one must have the mind to be conscience of position the writer didn't know the power of position until he was programmed by Coach Tracy. Nobody programmed the writer that the mind is what makes the person not even his mother, father, and his know it all brothers, or the learning institution of America. It derived from a former Slave owner the writer's great -grand father. Hallelujah and glory to God. If one want to know their future study your past. A beach ball doesn't stay under water forever.

The picture above is the writer at the age of 10 trying to pull a fish out of little triple T's pond, 'yes this is a pond that little triple T, dug with his hands. This was about thirty two Years ago after Tom death since Tom died in November of 1922, Tom left the family very well off, the farm was self contained.

The farm had fruit trees galore, a store bought house and a stock pond.

Tom last name was Topp he said the last name derived from being the top dog, in order to be a top dog one can't help but act like a top dog that's why Tom had the imagination of being the top Nigger in Fannin County Texas. 'Man he would boast about having the only stock pond among the Negroes in Fannin County Texas.

After Tom death Josie mother Polly married some stray from Oklahoma who was just looking for a home to destroy, his principles served his idea logics. After the pond was filled up with mud from neglect, all the fruit was gone and the trees died from neglect

All the fences were down or gone from neglect, the well had dried up from neglect.

The house was falling apart from neglect and the family had lost over two thirds of the three hundred acres plus farm. As a result of ignorance or not knowing, the writer knows the reason but will spare you the reader the details.

The bottom line reads Polly married the man he got what was in the cookie jar, and left Polly crying wondering what she was going to do. The same wind storm that blew him in he caught the wind and rode it out in a dusk of glory. As Tom would put it a piece of trash has no base, that's why I worked so hard to build my family base History has plainly demonstrated that's ones' principle will surrender to reality that's the reality that's the typical American Negro.

CHAPTER 3

JUST WALKING LOOKING FOR FREEDOM

THE WRITER HAD A GREAT uncle by the name of Ruben Phillips who was a direct decedents of the Phillips, the Phillips who were in modern times a oil tycoon you know the oil of Phillips petroleum company this uncle Ruben who was denied his rights to heirs of the estate. Because of the label and curse that was bestowed upon him by his biological father. Ruben who was born a slave and was a slave for the first 12 years of his life he was about 90% white the writer met this Ruben many times they would set together and this Ruben would talk about the days of slavery. Ruben had a brother a white brother about the same age as he was the white brother stayed in the big house a very large mansion and Ruben stayed in the slave quarters. In modern day time these quarters would be known as what we called today as apartments this was a very large plantation it was so large it had streets so said Ruben Phillips. Uncle Ruben love to talk about his past it was like he was relieving pressure when he talked about the past. This plantation had well over a hundred slaves the plantation was so large it had it's own doctor something that was un- heard of on a plantation. Something that the average slave did not have so when the writer talked about the past he's talking about a well documented period in his bloodline. This Uncle Ruben was the brother to the writer's grandmother the mother 0f the writer's mother her name was Polly. Polly was not born a slave physically, Polly was trapped in the fruits of slavery that was past on down to the writer it was said that this plantation Ruben deride from was somewhere off the coast of Galveston TX. The original slaves that was on this plantation came from somewhere from the Carolinas Uncle Ruben mother's father was white uncle Ruben mother father was also her grandfather and also her great-grandfather What? Is this a surprise to you the reader, as one can see as we write this thing about child sexuality is not knew one can very well see it started right here in America in the days of slavery? It was legal then, what would the justice say probably it's okay it's the property of the owner anyway what's the beef it's just a nigger hello America. As we write it's a crime on our precious little kids but when Uncle Ruben mother was a child it was ok because she was from the quarters, the slave quarters that is. Now the writers guess that the reader is saying how this can be the mother having a father that's her grandfather and also her great grand-father. Let the writer explain or let the writer spoon feed you the reader that was the terminology used by white America when they knew something the poor old Negro didn't white America didn't understand that. The American Negro was denied education so let the writer go on and explain the terminology on how Uncle Ruben mother could have and did have the same man as her father, grandfather, and great-grandfather. Well it shouldn't come as a great surprise history has plainly demonstrated that white American males love to have sex with young girls it's nothing new as we will explain. It's just been swept under the rug for safe keeping it's only one way home that goes to explain why all chickens come home to roost. That's the only thing they know one cannot run from their shadow the white American males have a saying that young girls are fresh meat this crime of the white American males having the appetite for children it shouldn't come as a great surprise back in the day of slavery the negro slave was consider grown at the raw age of thirteen so the slave owner didn't look upon their negro children as people they were looked upon as property or an investment so therefore, one will try and get a return on their investment as soon as possible so therefore the American whites was killing 2 birds with one stone. They the white American were having sex with their young Negro children and getting a yield on their investment also. Now you the reader thinks with the writer if a girl as in the case of Uncle Ruben mother was 13 at his arrival her mother was 26 at his arrival, her grandmother was 39 at his arrival. They all had the same daddy and uncle Ruben father was his mother brother and was white don't you see now do you the reader see the picture as it was told to the writer. The writer always wanted to document this uncle Ruben used to like to tell about his past, Uncle Ruben once said while attending church service at the writer father church he asked the question Where is all the people? It was about 40 in attendance uncle Ruben said he could remember when he as a young child growing up as a slave it would be more people in attendance than it is here today. It would be well over a hundred people because master made every slave on the plantation go to church. Why would you let the master care more about you than you do yourself? When I was a slave the colored folks wanted to go to church now that I am free they don't uncle Ruben couldn't understand why. He just love church then after uncle Ruben gave his testimonial he would take his handkerchief out of his suit upper pocket and began singing the song I am so glad Jesus lifted me while singing the song he would just be waiving the handkerchief and would be really happy. He would thank his god and Mr. Lincoln for his freedom he would start to cry for his mother and grandmother then would say that god guiding him to freedom. Uncle Ruben was 12 when they freed the Negroes his mother was about 25 his grandmother was about 39 and his great –grand mother was about 54.

When Uncle Ruben got the news that he was free, he would have been playing with his little white brother, but for some reason, his little white brother didn't show up that day. Then for some reason Uncle Ruben's biological father told them they would have to leave. Uncle Ruben's mother didn't understand why because she was so content living as a slave on the plantation. So his father explained to them they could no longer stay on the plantation. He told them to gather up a few supplies what they could carry in a sack which was a corker sack and this were all new to them.

An ex-Slave once said that innate sense is better than bought sense, meaning education.

Could that be the reason Negroes owned more land in 1900 than 2009? The Negro know the voice of their creator, but don't know the voice of their Sheppard.

That's the reason they love, the one they should hate, and hate the one they should love.

A Negro is a disconnected race thanks to the fruit's of Slavery, the poor old Negro look forward to the day when it will be no night and eternal peace forever.

Julion DeHorney would work six days a week as a laborer on the railroad the seventh day he would walk twenty six miles, one way every Sunday to preach at a dual purpose one room Negro school just for the honor to be called a pastor. His head deacon was a ex-Slave by the name of Sheppard Marshall.

All Americans must have an appreciation for the past history, of the American Negro in order to have a true compassion for the present.

Opportunity is segregated, the Negro have been denied the fruits of America and the Negro fight helped other minorities think including women.

The Negro suffers because of the consequences of ignorance because they had been dependent on master, they didn't even carry food. They didn't even know what to get, so he the master told them they would have to go. You are free now, they really didn't' understand. They were in bondage so long they really didn't know what freedom was. So the impact hit them like a rock hitting their forehead. They started to cry as if someone had died or got killed. The white master guided them off the plantation like they were herding cows. Some of the old ones were too feeble to go so master told them they could stay. He said we'll pay you but you young ones got to go. And he verbally told them to get the hell off of my place. Uncle Ruben said he remember it, like it was yesterday. He said his father acted like he was mad. He never seen him act that way before. Uncle Ruben would go on to say that to this day is the reason I don't like to see a white man laugh. Because my father was always joyful and always happy and that day I knew after years of thought that it was just an act that he showed what he really was he ran his own son his own children off of that place just like they were dogs and for the next three years man we suffered. He told my great grandmother that she could stay because she was his cook. Uncle Ruben said that he didn't know that he would never see her again so he didn't even say goodbye. They left all walking, talking crying acting like chickens, which had just been ran out of the garden. We didn't know which way to go I was just following the adults. So we went one way and it was like we were going nowhere. We didn't know where to go. We had never been off that plantation. We had everything we wanted on that plantation. That's all we knew it was about midday when we left so when night fall came we all gathered around, the preacher started praying oh yes the preacher was right with us. when night fall came we didn't even have any food to eat then when the sun rose, the kids were hungry we didn't know what to do so we started walking some was singing, some was praying, and some was crying we walked up on this plantation it was very small and the preacher went and asked the man for food. The man laughed at us and told us that's what we wanted.

To leave to move on told us to ask Abe Lincoln for food. Uncle Ruben said he didn't remember exactly how many days it was before he ate because by that time we were in destitute finally, we walked and found this one place where this man said he could use some of the Negroes to work. That he would give us food to work but he couldn't use all of us he said hey there is too many negroes I don't have enough food he was a nice man that's when the negroes began to scatter. He kept the majority of us. But it was a beginning of a journey that would end in Ravenna Texas. Some of the Negroes moved on to Ivanhoe. During that time it was a lot that took place. The writer don't remember exactly how long Uncle Ruben said they stayed on that plantation. But it wasn't nothing like the Philips plantation. Uncle Ruben said ho, ho, man we had everything in that place we ate like white folks like the whites here in Ravenna. We didn't eat like you niggers. I didn't know what suffering was until I got to Ravenna. But on the journey to Ravenna we really had hard times. Uncle Ruben would go on to say that after we would leave that plantation but the writer's doesn't remember how long he stayed. Because for one Uncle Ruben didn't just sit down and talk because some one would come and interfere and

Uncle Ruben would start talking to the grown ups. Because when the writer would return the writer's mother sold eggs and butter to what we the writer call a rich negro bootlegger in Bonham Texas man this man had the money he had large trash containers one would be full of fifty cents pieces , one full of quarters, one for the dimes and one for the nickels. He would tell the writer to go get a hand full of nickels he lived across the street from Uncle Ruben and Uncle Ruben's daughter. Uncle Ruben was well over a hundred years old at this point. From 1954 down to 1960, the writer would see Uncle Ruben every Saturday. The writer didn't play with other kids because his mother was very protective of him but man how did the writer love talking to Uncle Ruben. He was 6'6 weighed about 200 pounds. The writer remembers how he would go over to Uncle Ruben and he would ask him to tell me some more about slavery Uncle Ruben would ask he would say boy what did I tell you the last time lot of times he would be sitting out on the porch in his rocking chair. He was well over a hundred little did the writer know he would write and tell about this the writer, didn't have a TV so that was his entertainment but other kids would be riding their bikes, playing marbles or just throwing rocks. I had to stay close to my mother's side because she didn't want me to get hurt. A lot of times the writer's mother would say he don't feel like talking he's old Uncle Ruben would say ho if it wasn't for Abe Lincoln I would have been a stud. You see that woman there she's good looking me and her would make a good looking baby because I'm a good looking man. The writer wonder as we write did Uncle Ruben think if he had have been a stud would he have been procreating a baby for his looks or his size. The writer wonders what did Uncle Ruben think was they wanting good looking slaves or big slaves all the writer can do is wonder. But Uncle Ruben said that he had never been to war on the white Americans level but he had been at war by just being a colored man that was his words. Because Uncle Ruben said he remember on their journey to Ravenna that they came up on this town, but Uncle Ruben couldn't remember the town because Uncle Ruben couldn't read but the town was somewhere in east Texas and the white folks were voting that day and Uncle Ruben and the ex-Slaves was on a journey to find work. They were still wearing their old shoes they were very hard on their feet the preacher was their leader they were really looking for food on their journey. Uncle Ruben said they met a lot of nice white folks that would give them food he remember one house that they went to and the white man told them to leave and I quote "you niggers get away from my house" we don't want you round here and the nigger preacher told those white folks all we want is some water can you please give us some water and they drank the water and he said he guess the white man thought they was drinking the water so hard that they was using the water for food and the white man asked them had they ate the answer was no then, he turned to his wife and said can we feed these niggers and Uncle Ruben said he didn't know how many it were and he thought it were at least 60 and the white woman sat a table outside and just a small amount of food and Uncle Ruben said he believed the lord multiplied the food they ate and they all got full and there was food left over and the woman gave us food when we left.. And Uncle Ruben said there are some good white folks. Getting back to the town they were in Uncle Ruben said they were just looking for food he had no idea about voting and didn't know what voting was and the preacher went right up to those white folks and a white man asked the preacher what he was doing and he said we going to do the same thing you is doing we going to vote today so one white fellow came up to him and he couldn't remember if he was the sheriff or not and he told him to get these niggers away from here. And the preacher replied no we is people we is going to vote today same as you white folks Uncle Ruben said he doesn't know what happened but the man shot the preacher dead and all those folks started to run and holler. And the white folks on horses started running those Negroes like they were cows. When it was all over it was a bunch of Negroes hurt and dead, including Uncle Ruben's grandmother. She was run over and trampled by a horse and died immediately some of the Negroes were hurt and could not walk so by the scattering of the Negroes we left the hurt behind. He never knew what happened to them they didn't even bury his grandmother he said son lord only knows what happened to those negro people and the bodies because we ran and never looked back. He think he was somewhere in east Texas but he did not know but they had gotten the news form other ex slaves that they was catching negroes and putting them back into slavery. Years later Uncle Ruben found out that they were building penitentiaries and the negroes thought they was putting them back in slavery in actuality they were because white America needed someone to pick the cotton. Uncle Ruben used to say that the white man heard them talking and said that Abe Lincoln took their cotton pickers and they were mad about that. After over three years Uncle Ruben and the rest finally, arrived at Ravenna Texas and a place called wildcat thicket. About three miles out of the town itself, they called it wild cat thicket back in the days of slavery during the civil war they were nothing but outlaws ex slaves and ex confederate soldiers who were hiding out in wild cat thicket. Because the people didn't have no homes and there were cedar trees and nothing grows around them and you couldn't see through them so they would hide in there because they didn't have a house or land. The ex confederate soldiers were deserters. Some didn't have arms some didn't have legs now they were white folks. Some of the ex slaves didn't have shoes on their feet because the white folks took their shoes when they freed them because the white folks were that poor there were even some Indians in wild cat thicket but we all got along we were one big happy family white folks black folks and Indians we ran up on this big black woman man she was a tough sister every other word she spoke was a curse word she had a little boy who father was the master. He was about 6 years old at the time and he was a tough little boy but he wouldn't talk too much but this woman would cook beans in a wash pot and would feed anybody and would make liquor and sell it for a nickel That woman was the writer's great grandmother she learned her trade from William Cantrell. She was 25 when they freed the slaves. And she was taught to believe there was a god by her master but when she met William Cantrell and bloody bill Anderson that would change her thinking forever. That was the woman that raised the writer's father. Her name was Hannah and she had a house that the master gave her for her son that's where my father and all his brothers and sisters were born. That's the only house they knew and from that mentality it still fuses the blood in the writer as we write.

Now you the reader think with the writer just for a moment of your time just what intellect do you think he uncle Ruben had after his experience. Yes you are ever so right; he had an intellect that was damage just like any automobile have after a wreck. Just like any mind that has been damage now what kind of genetics can he pass on yes once again you the reader are ever so right, he can only pass on what he has damage goods. Just like the Holstein cow one can only pass on what they have the poor old Negro is no different.

This here uncle Ruben did not have the opportunity to purchase a paint brush he could only pass on what life had led him too. The opportunity was still in the future in the form of hope and a wish, no Santa Claus affect here, just pure actuality.

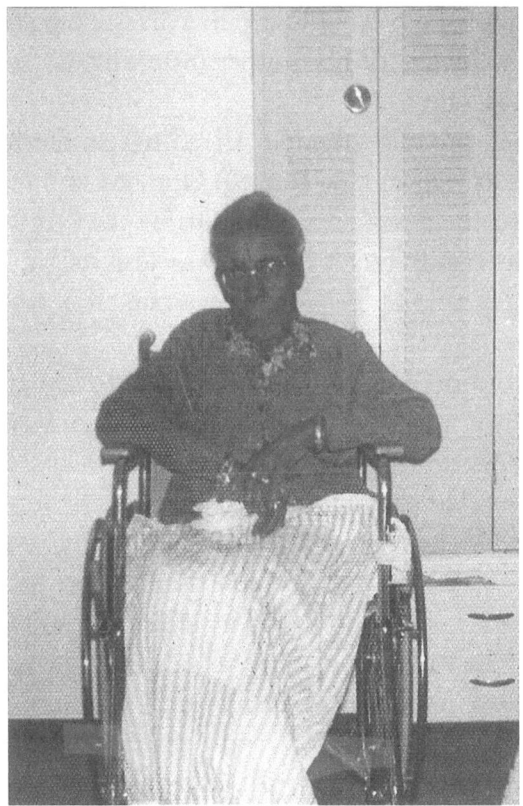

The picture above is the writer's grandmother, Josie's mother, she was born Polly Jones. She married little Triple T' as a teenager upon his death she remarried then her name became Polly Adams. Her life was a book within itself the writer will paraphrase her resume.

Polly was the half sister to Ruben Phillips; Polly's mother name unknown was born a Slave. She was the third generation father by her master, it was said she look like a white woman. Polly's father's name was Alfred Jones Josie would describe him as a African type short stocky black as a ace of spade it was said that he could cut a tree down with a axe before two men could saw a tree down. He had the label of being the best man with a axe in Ravenna TX. But was a dead beat dad. When Polly was born her mother died at Polly's birth or a short time afterward. Polly live here and there as a child her brother Ruben Phillips kept her until she was about ten, at ten she was so head strong she became a woman. Uncle Ruben use to laugh and tell about how Polly would sleep in a dresser drawer as a baby on the floor. The writer asked his mother Josie why didn't Polly's father take her and raise her?

Josie replied proudly grandpa Alfred have a family he couldn't raise her so Polly had to fend for self. One has to remember at this time in history, their was no C.P.S. not for the Negroes anyway, if another Negro family didn't help it was just tough; Polly was no exception to the rule of absolute. The writer has never seen Polly smile not once.

Polly was a mother at about thirteen, two years after that Josie arrived, and Josie was born in 1900. One can only wonder about Polly's age, Polly told the writer more times than the writer have fingers and toes that she didn't know how old she was. Polly would ask the writer boy how old are you? When where you born? Don't ever forget that because I don't know when I was born one has to understand the Negro had to fight for civilization and this is a prime example. Polly had two three Years of schooling because she could read and write. School didn't arrive in Ravenna until around 1890, for colored folks, but on the other side of the spectrum, they settle this territory so says history in 1836, guess what' that's when the school for whites derived. That's when the first roads were built guess who built them 'yes' you are ever so right probably some of Alfred Jones people. As a Negro we can only wonder, wondering is a way of life for the poor old Negro, wondering who we are, wondering how we derived, wondering how old are we, wondering why are we treated so bad, wondering why we treat our self so bad, but we do not wonder why we run off and leave our children. We know that we was program that way, wondering is a way of life for us it seems that's the life for the typical American Negro.

The picture above was Polly's favorite grandchildren to the left is Linda and Rose, Rose is the one holding mirth the baby as Polly would describe it. They had the label of approval from Polly the American Negro way of life derived from white America. The Negro had to have a leader, otherwise they would still be running around wild and naked in Africa and Polly's procreation was no different.

The writer remembers one time while visiting Polly's Rose, Linda and mirth the baby came over to Polly's and Polly replied well there come my little grand-children. Rose go get my pocket book, let me give my grand children some money we all lined up grand-children that is to receive our money Polly gave mirth, Linda, and Rose some money when it became the writer turn Polly said I have nothing for you, the writer didn't understand the writer's mother got mad and said lets go then, the writer mother told the writer that Polly would never give you anything, so don't ever asked her for nothing. The writer's mother would go on to say don't ever beg anyone for nothing its' more power in taking than begging. The writer can't say that Polly didn't give him anything because she gave him advice to keep up with his age. She never hugged him or showed no love she was just Polly, one can't give what they don't have that would be the same as one swimming where there is no water.

The Negro was programmed with fear, not love, the Negro don't understand that love conquered fear that's why education was not included in the Negro program the Negro was program to be separate and uneducated. The last time the writer saw Polly was around 1969, Polly told the writer to go buy her some snuff, snuff is a smokeless tobacco the writer obeyed Polly.

Upon returning with the snuff the writer handed Polly the snuff, and Polly replied 'you take that right back up there where you got it and get the biggest container you can find and the writer replied 'yes' mam' and obeyed. The writer heard Polly say that she had been dipping snuff every since she could remember she said she was so little she couldn't climb in a chair so she would set on a cigar box and dip snuff. Polly died around 1978, age unknown but a good guess would be around ninety.

Mr. Charlie Hill who visit the cemetery where Polly is buried said he had never seen any flowers placed on Polly's grave and he goes very frequently like every week. The poor old Negro would say fruit don't fall to far from the tree meaning, one pass their genetics on down, if one want to know their future just study their past that's the typical American Negro.

CHAPTER 4

LOOKING FOR PEACE AND OPPORTUNITY

AS YOU THE READER CAN very well see the poor old Negro had no comfort zone. At this point in life the poor old Negro comfort zone was embedded in slavery. Unlike their biological brothers and sisters the American whites, who could very well explain what a comfort zone was. That is why the poor old Negro cling to religion they are seeking a comfort zone. In reality they are not excepting actuality that's goes to explain why the poor old Negro sang redemption songs. The writer's great grand father was ever so right when he told his slave Hanneh and the mother of his son that she had not the slightest idea of what freedom was. In actuality freedom means the reality of surviving, surviving means the reality of preparing in essence it means the one who is prepared has the best chance of surviving. And what rate of surviving that goes into the genetics pool also that is the law of inheritance. One can only inherit what lies in their genetic pool that is the law of nature; one can't sneeze and chew gum at the same time. The same with one can't swim where there is no water or one can't swim without jumping into the water just think America the mind is what make the person. Now we are at the crossroads of religion one can very well say one's theology is as good as another the writer know the reader will agree with that because there is no present of actuality only the presents of reality. One can only say were life has led them but one cannot say were life will lead them. The same as one can believe what they want, but the facts will always remain the same and religion is no different. I the writer have never heard anyone down religion that's because of the fear of the unknown everyone wants to be on the safe side. Everyone gets a since of value when they talk about their religion I assume the slave owner would be no different history tell us that Columbus came over in 1492, and got credit for discovering America' America was already here it wasn't some lost ark. It was occupied as we have been told by the red man, but it wasn't until 1562, which is 70 years later before the slave trade started and history tell us that America was founded on a religious belief. And that's the key word belief so that would tell us the writer and the reader that whoever came to America was looking for a better way of life. That's so simple say's Mr. Walter Briggs who had a 2nd grade education no one is going to leave a table of food and go looking for food. In actuality that would be a fool since the bible tells us that a fool hates understanding and the American who discovered this great land were no different. If one is thirsty they will look for water so if one is uncomfortable with their present they will look for a better future. Isn't that the reason one goes to college to gain information yes they would look for a better opportunity; opportunity is the key word they were looking for a better opportunity and that of the slaves. The slaves only had one choice to do as they were told or die that were the only opportunity they had a very slim opportunity. The American whites had the opportunity to seek find and destroy. So, before one criticize the poor old Negro take a moment and evaluate the poor old Negro circumstance, because the poor old Negro made what is called circumstantial decisions that is pure and simple. As the poor old Negro would say do or die that's; the opportunity of opportunity. History has plainly demonstrated that the poor old Negro has gotten no help at their arrival as we write opportunity would be the key word. The poor old Negro was a basket case at the beginning and still a basket case as we write. The American whites have a saying about the poor old Negro; he's saying the Negro will not progress unless they are spoon fed. Meaning that they are slow, meaning that they are very slow, meaning that they are retarded, meaning that they are impaired when one that is impaired one have doubt where does doubt derive from doubt derive from not knowing. And not knowing is the most dangerous spot on the universe. And that is exactly where white America wanted the poor old Negro otherwise, that spot would have not been available for the Negro. Because white America was the one who put them there because the poor old Negro was created by and for the American whites history had plainly demonstrated that. Where did not knowing come from? Not knowing come from the lack of information, information comes from opportunity; opportunity was out of bounds for the poor old Negro. For example, Jerry Jones who is an American white and the owner of the Dallas cowboys and the writer is about the same age. The writer being a poor old Negro did not have the same opportunity if we did not have the same opportunity meaning we were not on the same playing field meaning we did not have access to the same position, and position is the greatest spot on the universe. Mr. Jones roots goes back the same as the writer's but in different position for instance, Mr. Jones people was not incarcerated unlike the writer's so upon the arrival of each individual we both started in different positions opportunity was available for Mr. Jones. It was not available to the writer or one can just say it was denied or rejected by this here America so, naturally the results are different one must remember one is what they think it's all about mind power, since the mind is what make the person. Mr. Jones was thinking about his future when the writer was just trying to exist in the present. Remember the writer's uncle Ruben Mr. Jones do not or did not derive from that type of pedigree the writer was reading the same books Mr. Jones was reading 10 years after Mr. Jones had read them so one can very well say that Mr. Jones had forgotten about the information he had read when the writer received it. The writer coached Mr. Jones boy Steven when he was about 12 years old. The writer went out in the hood and gathered -up under privilege Negro children in Little Rock Arkansas. Trying to give a helping hand and since the writer had a son the same age, the writer stumble up on Mr. Jones by accident. But it was a plan by Mr. Jones the writer gained a lot of knowledge by that experience of genetics.

By that experience the writer learned quickly, that Mr. Jones son Steven was born to be a leader. He was further advanced mentally than the Negro children. Mr. Jones son wanted to be a leader. On the other side of the spectrum, the Negroes children just wanted to play grab ass and act their natural innateness. That's derived from their genetics that is the results of the fruits of Slavery; the mind is what make The person.

Can one expect the same results from both parties? So, in other words, one cannot compare both as equal because of the starting position. Now can you see how important position is now? Do you the reader; agree that position is the greatest spot on the Universe? And not knowing is the most dangerous spot on the Universe for instance Mr. Jones was gaining information at the University of Arkansas while the writer was denied and rejected that opportunity. The writer was trying to spell opportunity and gain information on just what an opportunity was. What part did religion have to do with this positioning of the mind? Let's take a look and see just as the first ship load of Africans came to America the writer's great -grand father wrote that they the Africans were rounded up like stray cows would be rounded up they were in their Native land running wild and naked. They were rounded up and driven to a holding pen to be loaded on the ship the owner of the ship was a very religion man. He was so religion that he named his ship good Jesus please, you the reader do not get mad a the writer get mad at history the year was 1562. Did the ship owner load the Africans up for himself since he was a religion man? Was he trying to help the poor old Africans no' his ship was for hire meaning he loaded up the cargo for a profit and he wasn't on a mercy mission.

So did the Christians condone or condemned Slavery? We will let you the reader decide or have history already decided. Well one can very well say with not condemning Slavery the Christian religion started to put up a line of demarcation, for the haves and the have not's and the Africans were brought over here to be a mortar for America.

The first load Africans that arrive here in this here America on this ship Jesus didn't arrive here to hold a prayer meeting they came to build a America and to continue on to be an endowment as we write. What other purpose did they come for the intent wasn't the opportunity for improving the African lifestyle the intent was to better white American way of life? History says that 20% of all Slaves lost their life in route to this America; they call it the expense of doing busines. The 20% was just thrown overboard history says the conditions were so bad that one could smell the odor for miles before seeing a Slave ship. At all Slaves ports in this here America during the peek of Slavery one can only imagine in their wildest dreams the conditions, was so bad they unloaded the ship's cargo they would just take the dead and throw them overboard. Bodies would be every where the ship would be knocking bodies to get to the dock, the human bodies was just trash.

Now just what mind set do you think the African had upon their arrival? Do you the reader think in your wildest dream that they were ready to go to Princeton University? So what type of mentality do you the reader think those Africans had? Was they ready to gain knowledge or were they horrified, being horrified would that develop an impairment? Where was the religious sector at this point? What was their position at this point? History has plainly demonstrated that religion was not around to help the African; in fact it was over 200 years before the Christian religion derived For Slaves.

So, one can very well say history has already demonstrated that the Christian religion that was brought to America was segregated one can believe what they want but the facts remains the same. The facts will always rule so one must surrender to truth the fact will pave the way for truth, so by being segregated this here Christian religion was very selected. Because the Christian religion was out of bound for the Africans, so, one can very well say with the facts to back the writer up that the Slaves went over 200 years without a religion and another 200 years to get to the point were we are as we write.

The picture above is the writer's grandmother, the writer's father mother who's name was Mattie Glasper. She died when the writer's father was two Years old while giving birth to the writer's father baby sister who died a very short time after Mattie of child neglect. The writer great grand father said it best when he said the poor old Negro had no idea what freedom meant. Freedom means decisions the writer's great -- grandfather wrote and even tried to get a bill passed but failed in Texas to educate Negro in around 1880, said that if the Negro was not educated the Negro problem would only worsen. It seems that Dr. King agreed with the writer great-grand-father because Dr. King once said if white America stop and wait on the poor old Negro it would take the Negro 10,000 year to catch -up at the rate the Negro is pacing themselves.

Mattie Glasper was a full blood Choctaw Indian who got caught up in the fruits of Slavery that would be explain fully in another book about the DeHorney's. Mattie is buried the same with her baby daughter and a son by the name of Thurman in the same cemetery as little triple T and Polly somewhere one guess is good as another. Mattie gave birth to fourteen children fathered by William DeHorney. William Dehoney was born as a Slave, as all Negroes he suffered a developmental disorder thanks to the fruits of Slavery. William didn't have enough intellect to know he was suppose to love his wife as himself, to him she was just a piece of property. Not knowing is the most dangerous spot on the Universe, William can only be thanking the fruit of Slavery for that. We the writer can only wonder, about Mattie and her Offspring's resting place may peace and love be upon them.

CHAPTER 5

TIME DON'T CHANGE

THERE WERE NEVER A FINER parable when the writer's great grand father wrote, that time don't change only the events of time change. History has plainly demonstrated that. All one has to do is think and while you are thinking get an understanding. Just think how many thousands and millions of people have died for fighting for their religious beliefs which is contradicted to what they teach Jesus is love god is love but yet and still history have provided us with facts right here in this country of our America where America have killed people for what they believe because they didn't believe like they wanted them too. The red man is a good example history has plainly demonstrated that. That's the religion that we are talking about that is the religion that was kept from the slaves. All slaves for over 200 years they were programming their mind for a future use. You do as we say or suffer the consequences and it had the backing of the Christian religion, the Christian religion is very violent history has plainly demonstrated that with slavery. Not the writer the writer is only writing about history just straight and plain. That is why America believe in Santa Claus because of the psyche power. America benefit off of Santa Claus the Christian religion have the same effect as Santa Claus they preach one thing and then turn around and do another all, in the name of Christian religion. The Christian religion tells you what when and how to believe then turn around and do another. All one has to do is think. There was no finer parable when Jesus said a tree is known by the fruit it bears. This here America has produce it and backed up and supported by America's Christian religion. Now when one want to emulate their problem by killing wouldn't one say that there state of mind is in a primitive state of mind. Is that love by killing? Do the killer understand that the person they kill, that person is somebody's child? Possible a mother, possible a father, an uncle, a nephew or cousin it's just goes on down the line. That is someone they love one that they are taking the live from they are depriving them to their right to the tree of life where is the love. Who ordained them to be masters? There is only one love, or do they have a problem with reasoning God is love. Now you the reader should be getting a clear picture on how the slaves had to be impaired to exist under such conditions. And or in order to be successful in building this great nation, a nation we so love a structure is no stronger than its support. Anything that is successful it has to have the backing of a support group America is no different. In the case of America, America had to plan and build its support group that is why America created the poor old Negro. History has plainly demonstrated that support do not come automatically that's why the slaves had to be program to be and endowment. That is why America uses the poor old Negro to try and secure their future because all good things must come to an end. That why the impaired Negro is so important to America yes white America wants to keep the Negro impaired. History has plainly demonstrated if America uses the same formula they will get the same results it a proven fact. The dysfunctional Negro is looked upon by white America as an endowment the same as any root of any tree. At what point have the poor old Negro been helped for their illness? As we write none, instead they have been blame for being the cause of their impairment. Can you the reader imagine that in your wildest dream? Imagine a machine maker inventing a machine in return the maker of the machine blame the machine for it's malfunction. Well that is exactly what white America did they white America go out and procreate or plant the seed for the making of the American Negro and then blame the American negro for their being. Columbus came to America in 1492, and got credit for discovering America the land was occupied by the red man but it wasn't until 1562, before the first ship load of slaves came to this here America What do you the reader think the foundering father was during in that seventy year period? Yes you are ever so right they were planning and drawing up strategy on just how they were going to get farm workers for the land that they were going to take from the red man. One can see very plainly that the founding father didn't rush into anything history has plainly demonstrated that white America thought before making a choice from that choice it became a habit, from that habit it's became their character on how to oppress since the spirit thrives on what, one feed it, and spirit is the real self. The founding fathers, slowly studied their plan for nearly 70 years before deciding to go into African and catch the nomad African while running wild in Africa. The nomad African had an impairment at the beginning otherwise, they would not have been running wild and naked. Seventy years is a life time for many. So one can very well say that some of the original planner did not live to see the tree of slavery bloom. History has demonstrated that the founding fathers did not rush in nor did they forget about what had happen in 1492. Nor did they forget what happen in 1520, because they were exploring not like what they teach the poor old Negro to forget and move on. White America know very well if it wasn't for yesterday it would not be no today history has plainly demonstrated that with the yellow skin of the American negro. The yellow skin is not only a reminder but, also a reflection of what is and what once was the truth will set one free one can run but, one cannot escape their past. The poor old negro was taught to obey white America, to do as they were told not to do as white America did if white America use that logic themselves when a fruit tree bear fruit in the summer we are thinking of a peach tree which bears fruit in the summer. Now if one didn't believe in the past, once the fruit tree bears its fruit one would cut it down then use it the tree for barbecue wood wouldn't they? No that's not what happens they use the tree as an endowment, the same with the American Negro. White America do not want the negroes mind to advance they white America want the negro mind to stay put in place to worsen to be known as a stagnated mind not running as a stream of fresh water. Why? Because they white America want the Negro to remain in their impaired way if one change everyday that will be against the norm for white America. If one change everyday how can that peach tree grow up to bear fruit? Think America if one pulled up the tree everyday and plant another one in its place, if you forget the tree and don't nurture it where is the logic behind that. The same logics with the Negro, when they freed the Negro in1865, they white America just put the Negro out they didn't prepare the Negro for freedom they just put them out. Some of those Negroes didn't even have shoes on their feet but they put them out they didn't care it was said that Abraham Lincoln said Negro root hog or die. If you do not understand what root is that means dig, a hog that is not properly nourish digs into the ground looking for certain mineral to satisfy their taste buds if a hog is not properly nourish. That was said to be the advice then president Lincoln had for the American Negro that was the only help the Negro received. That was the only help the Negro got for their impaired vision or their impaired mind. But it took white America seventy years to come up with a plan. But the poor old Negro didn't have sixty minutes to transform, they the American Negro had to transform immediately. I guess one can say that is the reason the Negro is an experts at the game of transition, because the poor old Negro have been at transition ever since their arrival.

The picture above is Mr. Walter Briggs, and the horse is daisy, the horse was a loyal servant for over 20 Years. Mr. Briggs is the father of the co-author Louise. Louise was the fourth generation born on this eighty acre farm; it was a gift from their formal Slave owner.

As you can see the horse is pulling the plow, before the horse was available that was a job for the Negro despite having only two years of education Mr. Briggs built two homes he was program to be self contained. When the Slave owner own the land the land was very valuable to America but once the Negro obtained the land the land immediately lost its value to America then once the Negro gave the land away or just left it the land immediately once again had a value. Now what message is that sending to the world? Yes you the reader are ever so right to keep the poor old Negro as a servant. That's the very reason this chapter is name time don't change my friends it is impossible for times to change. It is the events of time, that only change since all events come from a supreme mind that explains why the mind is what make the person.

The writer asked Mr. Briggs why didn't he leave the country farm for the city, Mr. Briggs 'replied "well Jun I will tell you right now, I am Walter Briggs here, wherever I go I will still be Walter Briggs." In essence, what he was saying that it's the conditions that dammed the soul and one soul is determined by their inheritances. One can change their attitude but not their soul that's the law of nature, which was inherited from the unknown. Mr. Briggs would go on to say life is like a marriage it begin with a choice, choice derives from a decision and that decision is the most important decision one will ever make that decision will determined one's future. A decision can change the quantity of a person but can't change the content of the person. The content derives from the soul and the soul derives from the existing conditions. One can take the 80 acre land the Briggs was born on and cannot contain it on a city lot. As Ida Bell Gilmore [Sis] would say I am what I am and be thankful.

CHAPTER 6
BRILLIANT MIND PROCREATE WITH THE IMPAIRED

I GUESS THE WRITER CAN SAY it's time to get off into history and ask the question. The plain facts what would inspire an individual to go back and interbreed with a dysfunctional person or impaired person? We the writer ask you the reader to explain that to yourself. What would be the logics behind a man going breeding with a mentality disturb woman? What would be their logics? Would it be power? Or would it be that they are trying to growth their own human mental machine? What would it be, would the father, be proud of his offspring? Just where does the logic lie? But yet and still, America looks down on the poor old negro of today by continuing to perpetuate at the rate they perpetuate we are talking about the lower class negroes, yes its negroes that have progressed they have made tremendous strives with the help that they didn't received. White American have had help every since they came over here on the mayflower. But not like the poor old Negro that came over on the original ship Jesus. There was two different ships and two different logics, behind each load of cargo, the only thing each one had in common each one came to perpetrate but one ship came to enjoy and prosper but on the other side of the spectrum, that ship Jesus came to serve and be an endowment for future America. One can very well say that the mayflower when it departed for America it was blessed. But when the ship Jesus departed from African it was a curse restored upon it. Well one may asked why? Lets take a look at history and history produces facts on the mayflower ship people was let to bring goods over for one they brought their gods they had beds to lay in they had restrooms now on the other side of the spectrum, the ship Jesus that was a side of hell, no one want to experience. One can only imagine on the ship Jesus some of those people were praying just to die. Just imagine you was naked, they the Africans they could only bring their color and their emotional state of mind, you was chained you came on board you was chained to the side of the ship feet chained to the bottom of the ship standing up like any boxes of cargo. That was the start of survival for the black African no chair to set down one was standing up, was not free to move about no restroom, were in complete darkness. White America pack all they could get on that ship it was said it was packed so tight, it was like sardines in a can. Let the writer remind the reader it was said they lost 20% of the load they would say that was the cost of doing business. So they added extra cargo to make up for the loss, So where did the African sleep they slept standing up so where did they use the restroom they use the restroom standing up in place. Just like cows on a cattle truck think about that. Don't forget they where on this ship Jesus the man was highly religious who own the ship Jesus but yet and still he the owner let the slave handlers who was white raped the African women. Many got impregnated on that ship. Do you the reader; think they wash the women up before they raped them. Or do you think the white American males washed themselves up we the writer will let you the reader decide for yourself. This religious captain just turned his head to what was happening and that was the beginning of things to come. Now if one just remembers that if one doesn't know their past they will only have an uneducated guess of the future, it was a long journey from the shores of Africa to the shores of this here America. It was said the poor African was chained below deck for about 2 week before the African was able to go top side. They were so weak they couldn't stand some had to learn how to walk again one can only imagine it was a long journey. Every time the writer see's a cattle truck moving down the highway that reminds the writer on how the Negro derive here in this here America. That is the very reason why white America do not want to bring up past history; the truth will come to light. They white

America call it access baggage, they white America will quickly tell you the past is the past take this moment and move forward. They even got the poor old Negro saying let sleeping dog lie, because the dogs might wake up mad and want to bite. Just what logics did the ship hands have by raping those nasty Africans? The poor old Negro would say about the mentality of white American ship hands once they got by the smell they were home free. One can very well say the ship hands of yesterday could easily be compared to the long haul truckers of today. Or just your average John or Joe Blow for an experience, on skid row in any city of America. What drives these people to that kind of experience heaven only know the writer does not have the conclusion. Could it be power? Could it be loneliness? Or is it their mental acceptance whatever the answer is the answer lies within their mental conception. The poor old Negro would describe it like this it's just the dog in them, [WHOOP WHOOP]. Now by procreation from those two bodies the Africans and the ship hands who was the so called white American that blood line that they created will last forever so-says science not the writer. History has plainly demonstrated that there is cause and effects to everything humans are no different. Just as all chickens come home to roost it's their mental capacity that guide them home it is the force of their spirit your spirit is the real you. One choose what they think one cannot choose what's not available. So one can very easily see for self that the poor old Negro at the rate of 99.9 % of their procreation was procreated by a psychopath. And to exist as psychopath history has plainly demonstrated that. That's sad to say but one may believe what they want but the facts remain the same. This shouldn't come as a shock or a surprise to you the reader, the writer's grand father wrote this in the 1880's that if the poor old Negro was not educated there problem was going to worsen. In essence, its not only the negro problem its American problem for instance, it's a white American family who lives across the street form the writer who has a three years old daughter who still wears pampers but she can talk so well that she makes sentences and tell you what she want and the grandparents will tell you how smart the little girl is but as we write she is still in pampers. Do you the reader get the point that the writer is trying to explain? So one can very well say if one bow down, lie down, walk and exist as a lot lizard it can only procreate the same now let the writer move on. We all know why one cannot swim where there is no water just remember that scientist's say one drop of blood will last forever. In essence, what they are saying that the one drop of blood from a psycho will run forever in procreation and forever is a very long time. That would go to explain why in this here America we have people who rape people, who kill people, who eat people, who rape their own children who kill their children who procreate children by their own children. And who looks down on other people as if they were more that is the mind of a psychopath my friends. That is the one who created the American Negro since the mind is what make the person. Hello America as the poor old Negro would say how is you? Now can you the reader just think it all started, for the poor old Negro on this ship call good Jesus lets use the parable from the bible what was will be. Christians love to use this parable I am the same today, tomorrow, and forever history has plainly demonstrated that America is the same way. Just where do the logics lie, behind that parable all one has to do is think so would it be fair to ask the question, where does normality lie within the American Negro? Since the poor old Negro was created by abnormal people the black African and the psycho white American. So just where does this normal character come from that white America wants within the Negro. Does it exists or can it exist? Does it lay in the penitentiary or does it exists in education? We the writer will let you the reader decide, by the laws of inheritance if one use the same genetics one will no doubly get the same results. There is no better proof than facts, the roots of slavery by - passes education and go straight to the penitentiary history has plainly demonstrated that.

CHAPTER # 7

WAR IS NOT THE ANSWER

FOR EXAMPLE, THE CIVIL WAR was the greatest war that were ever fought in America over 650,000 lost their lives for what. Does killing ever solve anything? What about love, the Christian talk about since this here America was founded on Christian beliefs the poor old Negro is still looking for that love just where is the love. We the writer understand that there is only one love the writer will ask the question Did Jesus put the love in some other place on the way to Africa? Jesus is love, where there any love on that ship Jesus? Just where were the love shown for the Africans? Was it left in Africa to be used at a later date in the meantime, the African were going through pure hell to get to this America.

It was programming the soul of the poor old Negroes yet, to be created we the writer is still trying to find that love. Was it left in Africa trying to recruit more Africans to be used for white America please will someone find that love for the poor old Negro, because they need it now right here in this America.

The writer is very confused here since the owner of this here ship loved Jesus so much until he name his precious ship good Jesus. The man was so religious but it was said he gave up his religious belief to side with the psycho he had working for him. Before that ship docked at the American shores he the owner indulged in raping these African women all principles will surrender to reality. So, the name the good Jesus didn't mean a thing to the African that's the value of hope and by raping the wild Africans if it was many disease to be had he caught it too. He then spread it to his precious white women since penicillin had not been discovered. He forsaken his love for his Christian beliefs history has already demonstrated that.

The writer is trying to find a wrong that was done that turn out to be a right or a crime that was done to be better for mankind. There was no greater crime that was committed upon that ship Jesus but white America still want the poor old Negro to believe. While the facts speak for self at this time the writer would like to thank his master for this information. The writer father said many times, that the information was the yellow skin of his body it serves as a reminder of the past. The writer's late father said many times in his lifetime 'that it was a crime and a debt that the poor old Negro had not been compensated for." The writer's father would go on to say before horses came to America guess who were the horses yes' you the reader is ever so right it were the poor old negroes. The writer late father would go on to say the writer will quote him 'you know of all the things the poor old Negro have done for this here America And the white Americans has never given the nigger thanks not once have they said thanks." Yes the poor old negro had to serve as a horse until the horse arrive here in this America, pulling plows, wagon etc…one can very well say that the poor negro was just a human horse. They were slaves and they done everything imaginable, have the white man baby and serve as sex slaves. Anything that is imaginable that was the job for the Negro slave. Anything that is imaginable it was done to the poor old Negro that was the purpose of the Negro to serve and perform oh how they done that history has already demonstrated that and history don't lie my friends. It was all done in the name of progress for the progress of white America, the Negro serve and performs as a mortar for America. The writer's great grand father wrote, that in the planning stages for America whites America was hoping that the Negro we the writer is talking about a cross between the African and the American white which produce the American Negro.

The American whites was hoping that the original negro was sterile like a mule, which means they couldn't procreate oh how wrong they were and that also shows the reader the value or power of hope.

The writer do not know the facts about that but the writer looks to his great grand father for his expertise since he wrote 18 books and publish 9 and his genetics runs back to 1723, as a slave owner. He was a former slave owner himself, and a father of a slave experience is one's best teacher. Since America was supposedly founded on religious beliefs the writer can quote the bible. The bible says one cannot serve two masters they will love one and hate the other, that is the same with logics, logics is caught between the positive and negative when one is dealing with people what's good for one doesn't mean its good for the other meaning there is two side to a coin. There is a head and a tail to each coin the same with any tree there is a top and a bottom. There is to sides to everything including right and wrong. So just where are the logics when America lay claim that this here America was founded on Christian beliefs the proposition would be whose belief? Well history has plainly demonstrated that it sure was not the belief of the African, and once the poor old Negro was created they was born of ignoranance they didn't know head from tail they had no beliefs. They had to be taught what a belief was, how to believe, when to believe, and what to believe and guess who were the teacher 'yes you the reader are ever so right the poor old negroes teacher were their biological father the white American males. If Christianity didn't have two sides there would be no need to explain the difficult situation that stand before Christianity. The unanswered question that stand before Christianity there would be no killing there would be no need to kill, if there was only one way and that goes back to the logics positive and negative. So there has to be something wrong with that concept, all one has to do is think. Once one thinks, wouldn't one come up with the idea that America was built on a lie. Just what is a lie? We the writer will let you the reader decide for yourself and to yourself. Yes we know the writer has used this phrase many times in this book, before the conclusion of the book this phrase will be used again. Great possible many times, a structure is no stronger than its support, and without that support it wouldn't be any structure. The Christian religion is no different, America is no different, America whites are no different, a belief is no different, and that is the very reason why a scenario must have logic 99.9% of the times Humans got their ideal logics from someone other than self.

It is not in the power of the finite mind to determine how or when the universe came into existence. We can only take it, as we find it, and assume that it has existed forever. But it is in the power of the finite mind, to determine when and where the poor old American Negro and at what time, the poor old American Negro was created. Why? Because the white American left a paper trail, as the poor old Negro would say all one has to do is follow a chicken because all chickens go home to roost. History has plainly demonstrated that with the yellow skin of the Negro, it is a reflection to their creator. Every since the deprival of the human race. One is or program to think a certain way its not until a person is enlighten by information that they question a scenario, and religion is no different. The Christian religion teaches one to believe not to question in others words; one is given the information on how to think, and when to think. The same as the poor old Negro was when they were blank or empty, but once their mind was program it became full. No matter what the logics were their minds were full with positive or negative, no doubt in the writers mind the original Negro mind was program to be negative and the facts stand with history. History and facts don't lie because they have surrender to truth. So just what made this here America religious belief so strong could it be isolation, quarantine power and position since position is the greatest spot on the universe. The writer will explain in facts and details, it is not in the power of the finite mind to determine and the actual facts of the existence of the power of religion but, it is in the power of the finite mind the power and position of the system of the Christian religion. Since a system is only that of a complex whole. To a blind person one can only believe and a belief derived from that of a complex whole since the individual can't see for self. For instance, the writer who is blind and that's a pure fact the writer who was meditating in his vegetable garden fell and injured his leg. He was told that he injured his leg on some bricks, but by actual facts the writer don't have any because the writer is blind by physical condition and can't see for self. And so the writer can only believe what he is told but, the facts remain the same they the facts remain that he is blind and unaware of actuality. The same as any blind person they can only be led to what too believe just as one can only say where life have led one, one cannot say where life will lead them and the Christian religion is no different. One can only say what they know for facts what the Christian religion is, and the rest lies within the power of belief that's a pure fact not a hypothesis. Since Hypothesis lies in the facts of possibility, and a possibility serve only a possibility at best, it's a life long battle of the ages a long fight with belief with this here Christian religion and the beat goes on as we write. The facts are real that the African didn't come to American backed up by their Christian beliefs so by dealing with pure facts how can anyone in their actual mind set of reality can say that this here America was founded on a Christian belief without how that Christian belief derive from. One cannot customize a religious belief then turn around and say a belief is for everyone what they are saying in essence is that the Christian religion was customize for certain people and in return the poor African was quarantine for their beliefs. The Africans was not supported by their own idea logics when they were brought too this here America, remember they were quarantine and isolated. They the African were put into the position of a complex whole remember a position is the most important spot on the universe, and position only serve that of a complex whole. So what has history actually demonstrated, by the laws of actually history plainly demonstrated that the Christian religion was segregated, because that was the only thing available. In this here Christian religion was available to a certain exclusive group of people that served and shared esoteric intellectual interest. So, now you the reader need to think with the writer for a moment, and while thinking with the writer think for self. You are a wild African running, wild and free in your native land, speaking with your native tongue the language were taught form birth you were free to use the freedom of the innate religion that you were innate with. Now you are caught isolated, and, brought to a foreign land upon arrival you were quarantine and stripped of everything, you possessed nothing meaning, You could no longer speak your native tongue, meaning you could not pray to your god, meaning you could not move about freely physically. Now just where is, freedom for your mental existence. Yes you the reader are right there is none. So if you are told what, when, how, and where to believe where is your choice. Yes you the reader are right again there is none, when one is told what to believe, how to believe, and when to believe there are no choice my friends. That was the choice for the Africans then, the poor old Negro was created to be programmed by being program they did not have the right of freedom of choice. So, America could not and was not founded on a religious belief as we were and is taught to believe. You see my friends, when one is taught what, when, and how that is not a choice. Choice is an act of choosing, power to choose, right to choose, meaning to have an option. Option comes from position the poor old Negro was not in position to have or make a selection, remember position is the greatest spot on the universe. The poor old Negro was kept in the position of not knowing and not knowing is the most dangerous spot on the universe. By not knowing the Negro did not, and could not; make a selection on which religion to choose. Just like any blind person, they are and were in the danger zone, without danger what else did the poor old Negro have. Wouldn't you the reader agree? That is why the poor old Negroes life have led them too where it is as we write, because 0f danger. Now wouldn't you the reader agree that not knowing is the most dangerous spot on this here universe? Wouldn't you the reader agree that if it was not for yesterday, today would not be as we know it as we write?

Education teaches us that one can't hold on to Monday and go too Tuesday at the same time, history has plainly taught us that. History has plainly demonstrated this here America led by this here Christian religion will try and keep the poor old Negro in quarantine from information and try to move into the future at the same time it can't be done my friends. Not under the sun we live under, as the poor old Negro would say, us colored folks get our help from above, it was not meant to be from the slaves ship to the white house its a no' no' it was not meant to be. As the writer said before, it is two sides to everything history has taught us that the Christian religion is no different. So one can plainly see, that this here America was not founded on a equal or just Christian belief the black wild African was running wild and free in their native land. So why anyone would go and captured them and take them to a foreign land and put them in quarantine mentally and physically for over 400 years. And make them part of the society. They was part of a free society. What was done to the Africans can't be duplicated, because America pulled up from the strength of that black man then, built a law denying another to have the same opportunity. But, let the writer remind the reader that slavery and Jim Crow existed over 400 years. And this here religious sector in this here America did not say negative words about the wrong that was going on for over 400 years. In the meantime, the religious sector was building and going too the bank at the same time, banking the money they reap from the fruits of slavery and dishonesty. A system was installing for the act never to be duplicated again so, America built a country as for what they wanted it to be at the expense of not knowing. And America is still reaping the benefits as we, write, the system is set up for the illiterates to serve as an endowment as we write. Everything is all good for the man with the plan, the man in position to make the system. If one is against that system people look upon that person as being negative, that is the way it is done in this here America. Its about the dollarism yes we are told that this here America was founded on this religious belief but, slavery contradicts that plainly if one thinks for self. The slaves were so dysfunctional as we were told by white America, but while white Americans were saying that, they were procreating with them at the same time. Yes the Christian religious sector saw it the same way, they probably would say there nothing wrong with being the father of a little nigger child. They looked upon that nigger child as a toy a pet and a property, remember they kept religion out of the hands of the nigger child for over 200 years. My friends we cannot and must not forget that in the meantime, while procreating that little nigger child there was never any child support benefits paid to the little child and their rights to any inheritance was also forfeited. That fate that existed then cannot be duplicated as we write because of the brilliancy of position in this here America. Position serves as a complex whole for the power structure the same as the mind serves the individual, the mind is what make the person. A position is what make the system and serves the system, one just can't go out and duplicate, the fate of the poor old Negroes biological fathers white American. A Position serves as the key to turn information on or turn off information in other words, one can just say if one has the power of position one can do what one wants. The power of position is the do's and don't of any system for example, the poor old negro can't go out and procreate a future generation without paying child support. Unlike their biological fathers, the poor old Negroes biological fathers' yes we are still talking about white America can go out and procreate with the poor old Negro and go to the church of their choice and have a blessing restored upon them. But, on the other side of the spectrum white America biological children the Negro males can't duplicate that instead; of getting a blessing if they don't pay child support they will get a great curse restored upon them. With the blessings of the Negro churches the curse, will be that of the penitentiary system. Is this even Steven? Because the Negro churches do not normally preach about this unjust law that was created too bless white America, and dam the soul of the poor old Negro. Now if the poor old Negro had receive their back child support 'hey' there would be no problem with the law as we know it as we write. So, why do white America criticize the poor old Negro for doing the same act as their fathers? Is this injustice? Or absolute ignorant the poor old Negro learns every aspect of life from white America Why? Because the Negro was created by white America and was taught every aspects of their being. So, if one follow the root system back too the original base they would find in all purity that the poor old negro is not responsible for their ignoranance remember the poor old negro did not place themselves in quarantine upon arriving in this here America. Remember the poor old Negro has been fighting for liberation upon arrival in this here great America; remember white America kept information out of the minds of the poor old Negro. Remember the poor old negro, had to fight for excess to education now, just where do the blame for ignorance exists if the poor old negro, was fighting not too be ignorant all while white America, was fighting to keep things as they knew it yesterday , today and hoping it would last forever. Now, by the laws of absolute truth wouldn't you agree that the problem of the poor old Negro began and still exist as we write with white America. That is a side effect of wanting and keeping one in ignorance or could we just say that is the fruits of slavery. One can let the chickens out of the hen house but, all chickens will come back home to roost, there was not a finer parable when Jesus said a wise man build on a rock and a fool on sand.

History has plainly demonstrated that white America was very wise and white American biological children the American Negro wanted and want to be just like white America. Now if white America was wise doesn't one have enough decency in their soul to know the poor old Negro want to be just like white America, So just why do they think all chickens come home to roost, why? That is what their soul was, and is built on. The poor old Negro paid a price too be where they are as we write there is no Negro, living in America as we write who don't want to be something just go out and ask them. Why don't you? They are the victim of circumstances whatever it may be Negroes had to fight just to learn how to read. The writer has heard stories about how the poor old Negro lost body parts for just wanting to learn how too read. Some lost their hand for trying to write, some lost their eye for looking at a book, and some lost their tongue for trying to read. For example, The writer knew an old man by the name of Taylor king who's father was a slave this Mr. King told the writer that his father told him, that it was a slave boy who was being taught to read by master's son the Negro slave had a book turned bottom side upward and was playing like he was reading the master caught him setting on master porch pretending he was reading. Master asked him what are you doing? The little slave boy didn't say a word the son tried to intervene, by saying daddy he do not know what he is doing cause the Nigger has the book bottom upward. Daddy one cannot read bottom upward, but little did master know that, and master replied I know that son but, I don't want you to teach the Niggers how to read because I the master do not know how to read. So just how much will this here Nigger be worth if he can read? So the master caught the boy and tied him up, reach in the Nigger boy mouth, master pulled out his pocket knife and cut the nigger boy tongue out. Then, master replied let this be a lesson to you and all the other Niggers on our plantation, if you don't know what this here Nigger is saying we don't know if he can read or not. Always keep the Nigger worst off than you are son don't ever let a Nigger take your place. What a price to pay for just wanting to read, whatever one find white America, wanting for the poor old Negro one will always find a tom following behind white America in agreement this sound like slick Eugene.

The picture above is the writer's niece Denise De Horney and the writers' son Coach J. R. DeHorney on the tricycle, if war is not the answer that leaves only love. Jesus said it best when he said you are either for me or against me, the poor old Negro does not understand through unity there is strength. Why? Because their neatness did not program them with understandings that's why a developmental problem exists for the American Negro.

CHAPTER 8

HATRED AND REALITY

THAT REMINDS THE WRITER OF a living experience while living in Yuma Arizona, working at a place called the federal compress It was a place in history that comes out of the twilight zone, it had six where houses and one water fountain and one rest room for the Negroes and one for the whites. One coke machine for the whites only, no cokes for the Negroes, all the supervisors were white. And all had problems reading the writer just graduated from high school and needed a job. So he took this job at this post slave facility, the writer were unaware this type of mentality still existed. But, the writer soon found out how inexperience could turn into experience, this Mr. Guy gave the writer a 6 digit number to a bail of cotton and was told to find Mr. Arkie for he could find this bail of cotton, Mr. Arkie was preoccupied when the writer found Mr. Arkie so the writer found the bail of cotton himself to save time. He took the bail of cotton back to Mr. Guy little did the writer know, that the piece of paper with the number on it Mr. Arkie was supposes to initial it. So when the writer got back to Mr. Guy he asked the writer just what is this? The writer replied this is the bail of cotton you wanted, Mr. Guy replied just were is Mr. Arkie initial? The writer replied I don't know Mr. guy asked were did you get this bail of cotton?: At the same time, this Mr. Guy had turn red and swollen up like a bull frog and the bull frog and looked the writer right in the eye and said 'As long as you are working for the federal compress don't ever do this again. If you do it again you will not be working here any more because you do not know what you are doing. You do as you are told or otherwise you will not be here you are to obey the one who have rule over you no matter how long it takes. You can't do my job so do not try and don't even think about it do you understand and the only answer that you can give and be accepted is yes sir do you understand? And the writer replied yes sir. This type of behavior was approved by the Christian community before slavery, doing slavery and after slavery it was and is approve by the Christian religion.

For instance, a lot of weight weighs very heavy on this here Christian religion, if one will look at actuality and not probability. For example, everything develops a root system the Christian religion is no different it cannot escape the laws of justice, just like right or wrong. No one has the right to kill another; the same with no one has the right to quarantine another, wrong is wrong and right is right. No matter who does it? The writer would like to think that Jesus would agree so if you the reader like Jesus you will love the writer. The writer's great grand mother was trapped by slavery, mentally and physically she produce a son that was a victim of slavery both never attended a day of school in their life. Hanneh grandson the writer father he had three years of schooling he could read and write. The writer mother had 8 years of schooling, the writer has a high school degree, the writer's son coach J. R. De Horney not only has a high school degree, but has two college degrees as we write. Now is that progress or what? From Hanneh to Coach J. R. DeHorney that is five generation now one can very easily see that is five generation of improvement. Each generation is continuing to develop a stronger root system, now if Coach DeHorney continue to plant seeds of prosperity in his students and children the results of the information that coach De Horney Received will continue to grow. One must not forget a structure is no stronger than its support, the writer would like to, think that coach DeHorney is growing a structure of success and like any structure it needs a support base. As with any base the base is the beginning of a root system, since the writer and his only sister came from the same root system he the writer will use his late sister may peace be upon her soul to illustrate the two different mind sets of the typical Negro. The writer' sister graduated from high school also, she only had one child a son Rev. C.D. Sweet he also graduated from high school. He has about two years of college; he procreated two sons as we write they are yet too obtain a college degree. What the writer is showing is how the root system of progress, was cut with this here C.D. Sweet the progress of higher learning ceased with that generation. In other words, life is like a foot race one must live to enjoy life the same with a foot race one must continue to walk or run to finish a foot race. Now with the writer side of the competition there has been a steady growth of a new root system, now on the other side of the spectrum, the writer's sister side the progress stalls with the 4 generation. Now a new root system must be developed, or started because there has been a process of stagnated growth with the structure. Remember, a structure is no stronger than its support, What the writer is trying to show is that one must steady growth and cannot have any lack of progress within the root system. The same can be said for this here Christian religion just where is the help from the Christian religion other than the belief system and all systems are the form of a complex whole, meaning one is bound to a complex idea logic. Meaning that when one is program by another that person, is control by another one's thought since the mind is what make the person. For instance, the writer will start with his great grandmother Hanneh her root system can be traced back to 1723, But , we the writer will spare you the reader the details and just start with Hanneh, the writer's great-grand mother. She was 25 years old when they turn the slaves a loose she was program, and control by her masters therefore, her life existence was preprogram for her meaning the system of this here America had a pre-condition plan for her the same with all Negroes otherwise, the poor old Negro would have gotten help for their conditions every American negro born in this here America, were developed for a purpose including Hanneh. Meaning the mind had to be damage in order to be successful. The original mind of the poor old Negro was damage to start with, the root system was put in place from that it perpetuated. The mind was damage by injury and a curse.

So when one know better and don't do better they are putting a curse upon themselves, for instance, when a person go get drunk and gets behind a wheel of a automobile that is a curse. That's the same when a child is not programmed to get a higher learning too be successful and they know that a higher learning is required to be successful, that is also a curse. It is one thing to be forced into ignorance but, it another thing to volunteer for ignorance, that is a mortar my friends. A mortar for the will of the oppressor, by now you the reader should have enough information too decide who the oppressor is so, why would any one be store a label upon themselves. By doing nothing for self one put a label on self, the poor old Negro had a fantasy of a person by the name of Whit Dumb, old Whit Dumb would set up and say I can't do that and old Whit Dumb didn't try to do nothing. Then he would put a label on himself. Why would whit dumb do that? One may ask old whit dumb would reply 'I' suppose to obey those to have rule over me so say the bible. The bible told me to do everything I do, that was the poor old Negro motto but once the poor old Negro seen daylight the poor old Negro was told that the reason they can't see daylight is because they are being oppressed so hard they can only see darkness. They see darkness as light but once they see daylight for self they will discover the difference between light and darkness. Now if a person want too volunteer themselves for darkness one can just say they are a mortar for a better America.

The poor old Negro was program to be against other Negroes not to be in agreement. Not to respect other Negroes or anything they stood for. The poor old Negro was program to believe that the Negro was their enemy the poor old Negro was program to love who ever was their overseer and to hate all Negroes at any cost. The poor old Negro was program to believe that whoever was their master that person, was God sent. The writer have had negroes even preachers, to tell him just that, saying that is why the bible says obey those who have rule over you. For that reason and that reason alone is why the Negro has been kept in darkness so long, to deny them the right to a rebirth. The poor old Negro was created to be inferior, to be impaired that is why they kept education out of the hands of the Negro. So one can very well say, and I'm sure you the reader, would agree that a person when trained is like any other person that is trained. For instance, a, fighter is trained too react as a fighter, an educator, is trained to react as an educator an impaired, person is trained to react as an impaired person. So, in order for each individual who is program to respond in a certain way, can only pass the genetics that lies in their genetic pool. And the only way that individual can escape their genetic pool is by rebirth. now let's say a father have two sets of children, one set by his white wife and one by his Negro slave, history has plainly demonstrated that the father will put all of his emphasis, on the white children. That is the power of position, and the force of his emotions, meaning he the father would do anything possible under, the sun in which we live for his white kids to have the pursuit of happiness. Now on the other side of the big house, where his little Negro children lie it's just the contrary, meaning they would be programmed to do everything under the sun to make their white brothers and sisters the precious ones. In other words, it would be all good and positive for the white children, on the other side it would be all negative meaning they would get what's left. Giving the precious white children the choice of what was left, if nothing was left the poor Negro children got nothing, that's the power of position my friends.

From the laws of inheritance. The precious white children was taught to have freedom from doubt, and was supported by their negro brother and brother and sisters, all w while the poor old Negro children was programmed to be inferior and they had the support from their father, mother, and white brothers and sisters. That is also the power of position, one is a positive and the other is a negative but, it's all about position. The position of the mind since, the mind is what make the person you are what you think, and you are the one who choose what to think by programming a person on what, when, and how to think that person will be controlled by another person thoughts not self. So what kind of complex will the children have? The white children would be self assuring in other words, they would be in control a goddess, and have the opportunity to be wise the poor old Negro children will be just that of a Nigger. History has plainly demonstrated that, with the result of the writer's great uncle Ruben Phillips. History has shown that the poor old Negro was programmed to be self contained. Meaning to show support for the label that was put upon the Negro, the poor old Negro would show his support and loyalty by placing a label on themselves and their future generation. A label is just a curse my friends, as the writer has said before, everything the poor Negro knows came from white America.

The picture above is the mother and father of the co- author, Mr. Walter and Guthrie Tate -- Briggs. The name Tate derived from her grandfather who was a full blood Cherokee Indian. Mr. Walter Briggs and Guthrie knew all to well about the reality of hatred that was in existence of their reality. Both were born in 1911, they were programmed with fear, despite the fact that they lived under Tyranny of hatred that surrounded them they still found the time for love.

Ms. Guthrie said she showed love and caring because she wanted to be love and cared for she had experience that I don't care don't have a home, history has proven that. If a person can't care about one thing they surely can't care about two. Mr. Briggs said he grew up in a time where people love to display hatred, and he remembered the time when a train left Hope Arkansas full of white's folks headed for Paris Texas just to watch the lynching of a Negro.

Those white folks headed for Paris Texas just to watch the lynching of a Negro. Those white folks were laughing and joyful and were just happy to be part of the event, they returned with some of the Negro body parts as souvenirs. That was an experience that would last me forever he said, I can only wonder how people can be so hateful.

Mr. and Mrs. Briggs raised seven children as one can wonder what is in Ms. Briggs hand it's a sweet potato they were digging to send back to Arizona to her grand children. Is that love or hate? Peace be upon their soul.

CHAPTER 9

HOLDING ON TO YESTERDAY

EVEN AS WE WRITE THE Negroes of today will tell their children what they can and cannot do in life. The family will pick out the ones they choose for success, and will program the majority to be a supporting cast to the chosen one 99.9% of the times. That's the way the typical American Negro does it, the writer has experience just that in his upbringing as an American Negro. It was no different from the days of Slavery, in the days of Slavery the Negro babies was told at birth, their future agenda, just like cows on any cattle ranch it was a business. The poor old Negro can only pass down what they have and the writer's family was no different they could not pass out genetics that was not in their genetic pool. So was this system that was used in this America right or wrong? From a business perspective it was a good business decision, from a moral perspective it was wrong. So just what did the Christian religion say about that since, this here America was founded on a Christian belief. Well the writer would say that history has already demonstrated what the Christian religion would say and have said. Would you the reader agree? Facts speak louder than words,

With the facts on the table, each root system is a knew beginning as with all new beginning. The beginning starts with what happen yesterday or in the past, or if one wants to be precise it starts with the present and immediately goes to the past. So, it is very factual, that the poor old Negro system started with the inner locking between the African women and the white American males it started with a fifty-fifty mix. White America want to deal with only the African part of the mix, history had plainly demonstrated that. As if the white male had nothing to do with the mix but sorry America your bubble has been busted. The American Negro was rejected, denied, and placed in limbo at birth. So, in actuality what else could the poor old Negro be accept inferior, it started with the sex act. Just what was the African woman thinking about while the Negro was being conceded? Was she thinking that she had the power? Or was she just happy having sex with the white American. Now on the other side of the spectrum, by actual facts the only thing the white male was thinking that he had the power, plain and simple. So what did the baby come here thinking? 'Confused' so the baby comes to America as a new born. What did Slavery do for their mentality? It worsen. At what time did her inferiority complex diminish? It didn't its still here as we write; at this point what part did the religious sector play? 'None' Just where is the love? It came in the form of hope and by the laws of reality hope is worthless. Scientist say one drop of blood will last forever, and forever is a long time. So, by the laws of inheritance American white's is part of the mix just as light is a reflection of the Sun. As would be with the yellow skin Negro is a reflection of their biological father white America. Not only do the poor old Negro have traits from their biological father the poor old Negro is not only a Negro problem it is also the problem of the biological father.

White America have plainly demonstrated that one cannot escape their past, as they have also plainly demonstrated that one cannot out run their shadow no matter how hard one try. One can or may turn from their shadow that is the only way they can escape their shadow. White America has always tried to live a double purpose life as old Whit Dumb would ask what you mean Mr. Writer. Well if one look at the facts they will see facts as they are and not as they want them to be. The facts are everything White America try and create everything in pairs, for example, religion, history has already demonstrated that white America will get up on Sunday morning and get ready to go to a prayer meeting and on their way to the prayer meeting then detoured along the way and take out enough time to drag a Negro if the position present itself.

They will dumped him into the River, burn his home and anything else that is imaginable and will continue on their way to church as if nothing happen. Once arriving at church they will get on their knees and pray but, in their prayer they will not mention the wrong they have done upon the poor old NEGRO. Now you the reader called that a dual purpose intent or mission this is history at work not the writer. History has provided the events, all the writer is doing is writing about the events. White America has demonstrated that the poor old Negro can build a stadium for an event but, the Negro can't perform at the event. For example, building War Memorial Stadium in Little Rock Arkansas but could not enjoy the stadium until the position of events changed. Now isn't that a dual purpose? Old whit dumb would say that the White American male is a dual purpose specialty. The yellow skin of the Negro provide us with that fact in the meantime, the white American male will call that light skin Negro black. Reaching back into the genetic pool, the poor old light skin Negro agree with white America and call himself black. Why? Because that's what white America wants, back in the days of Slavery the master would come out and greet his Slaves on a work day. And the master would reply, boy I'm sick today and their would be a Tom in the group that would reply 'YESS SIRR master we sick today. History has shown that times don't change; only the events of time Uncle Tom went under cover he has gotten sophisticated. They are now educated, a light skin Negro who call themselves black because that is what white America want. Saying undercover, the bible say obey those who have rule over you that's their logics undercover to justify that for themselves conscious they know all so well that they are not correct. But the poor old Negro was created to know their purpose the Negro sole purpose was to obey and to perform. And oh how they performed for example, the writer was working for a very wealthy white American who was a personal friend of Arkansas former Governor Fabus. The writer was employed as a truck driver the man name was Cooney, and one day the writer wife came to pick -up the writer along with his 8 year old son. This Mr. Cooney came out to meet the family, Mr. Cooney asked the son and the writer will quote him. 'Son what do you want to be when you grow up?' A truck driver the son replied. 'Oh no Mr. Cooney replied if you become a truck driver there is no margin for improvement you want to go to college an get an education." While inquiring you may decide what you will be replied Mr. Cooney. The writer said all of that to say this, at no point, in the life of the son did the writer ever mention to the son to be a truck driver. From day one, all the writer ever talked about to his son was about a college degree, so just where did the idea derive from? It derive from his in born senses meaning his genetics. The writer asked his son why did he say truck driver. Knowing all alone the writer wanted his son to be more than that. The writer's son replied Daddy I said that because I thought that's what he wanted to hear. You see my friends the reader, one's soul is already programmed if it's not refine by physical means its no different from any genetic pool. One must remember one cannot swim where there is no water. At what point, have the Negro mind been refined? The Negro mind must be refine from 1652, to 1966, from the first ship load of Slaves that derives here in this here America on this ship good Jesus, to total integration was there a time that the poor old Negro mind was refined, and the mind is what make the person. The poor old Negroes were created to obey and perform the refinement of the mind were not part of the equation.

All the poor old Negro ever wanted was to be accepted, by his biological father white America that was a no, no, since that meant being equal. Why didn't white American want the Negro equal? Was white America afraid? We will let you the readers decide or were they afraid to let the chickens out of the coop because the laws of nature states that all chickens go home to roost. The poor old Negro would say, white America do not want the stray chickens hanging around the big house that would give the wrong image of absolute. So, just why do you the reader think the poor old negro spent millions of dollars on hair grease to get their hair straight like white America. That alone demonstrate that the poor old Negro was not satisfied with what they had. Anytime any one try to refine themselves, which automatically explain that one is not satisfied with self. For example, if someone graduate from high school and do not go too college, that means that they are satisfied with the present, excluding some verbal's. The American Negro was created and programmed to satisfy white America. That's goes too explain why the poor old Negro will harm themselves in order to get a laugh out of white America that Negro will do anything to make that happen. Even if it means to worsen himself and cursing his future generation that is the very reason America is where it is as we write because of the dysfunctional Negro. Do you the reader realize the poor old Negro have not been help for their problem? Do you the reader realize that the poor old Negro helped build Harvard University? Not for themselves but, for white America, the poor old Negro help build a system that would turn around and form a complex whole on the poor old Negro. And that whole exists as we write and the poor old Negro is yet to receive help or compensation for that fate. The poor old Negro have a saying, that is if one don't know where they come from how do they know where they are going because, when one gets there they will not know they are there. That's so real, because when one see the media, young an old like white America media always, downing the poor old Negro for their do's and don'ts and by laws of nature the poor old Negro is not the actual problem. If one is politically correct for example, if one put an egg in a nest and the egg hatch into a chicken. Who would you blame the egg or the chicken for its being?

The poor old Negro didn't create themselves for example, if one procreate a child who is responsible for the up- bringing, including the education? Well, you are ever so right hello America as the poor old Negro would say how is you? The poor old Negro was not programmed to be politically correct, the poor old Negro once described life in this here America was like a segregated track meet. The Negro made the track, and was told they could compete in the track meet but, wasn't told that all the medals were for white America. As with any track meet, each step is an advancement to the finish line one must cross the finish line to receive their medals. So the Negro start the race all so good, but white America was in position to gnaw off the poor old Negro legs to give him a handicapped. And when the race is over white America would praise the white athletes for their brilliant effort and belittle the Negro for not having the heart, and the inability to compete. And most of all not having the legs to finish the race and no desire to win, that's the conditions that America's typical Negro exist in.

Here is an actual scenario, that the typical Negro has existed under the year was 1946-1950 in North Texas the town was called Ravenna Texas.

Or could we just say community. Because the family existed about 5 miles outside of Ravenna it was a family of six. The lady Josie was the niece of this uncle Ruben that we talked about. Her grandmother was an ex-slave Josie had 8 years of schooling, her husband Junion, had a 3rd grade education, his grandmother and father were Slaves. His grandmother came to that community by the way of Kentucky, in a covered wagon. The year was 1859, her master would become the father of her son Junion father. The master would become also Julian grandfather Junion was born in this community; he was one of 13 siblings. They bought a fifty acre farm in what was once known as wildcat thicket. As white America describe it the whites from this neck of the woods that is the white's called it fitting only for a Nigger.

You the reader can decide for self, what it was like or you can just use your imagination of what you do not want to exist in. For instance, if it rained you were surrounded by water the house was upon a hill, if it rained when you were in you couldn't get out. If it rained and you were out you couldn't get in, Julian was seen many times wading in water up to his chest trying to get home, during the civil war this part of North Texas, this served as a hide out for William Cantrell and his raiders alone with bloody Bill Anderson and Frank and Jesse James. Alone with deserters from the south and north cut throats and Choctaw Indians alone with run away Slaves until they became settle in. In other words, it was a no man land that's why the whites' called it fitting for a Nigger. The county which was Fannin County would not build what the poor old Negro would call a store bought road. It was what the Negro called a Nigger road, one can only imagine; Junion and Josie had three sons and one daughter the oldest at this time was in the navy or in college. The second son was either in the army or trying to find himself in Chicago, after he left the army he went to Chicago to try and learn the trade of a shoe cobbler. But once he returned after about a 90 day stay, he described himself as a hustler a career that started and ended in Chicago the girl was a pre teenager at this time and the third son was around six. They were trying to farm the land which the government allotted them about two acre of cotton and two acres of peanuts. One year they produce a bail of cotton from the two acres it was said Josie just cried and thank her god for the cotton. The bail of cotton was worth about a hundred dollars Jose cried out to her God saying thank you god, we can make it until next year off this one hundred dollars. Julion was also the country preacher, Julian built the three bedroom house they lived in he also built his barn. During this same period of time the U.S. Government, was building what the poor old Negro called store bought houses for the white folks. This was not available to the poor old Negro Why?

Because the Negro was the wrong color, one can just say that these government funded store bought houses were out of bounds for the poor old Negro. During this same period of time the State of Texas was building, what the poor old Negro describe as store bought roads to be politically correct they were called farm to market roads, these roads were also out of bounds for the poor old Negro. Julian tried to no avail to get the farm to market roads in the Negro community There excuse to Julian was it was not enough money to build roads for the Negroes. Saying white America had more farm good than the Negro, so therefore, white America needed the roads more than Negroes. Julian drew up a plan and showed the authority on how they could serve some of the Negro with the farm to market roads. Because the roads was put where there was no one living and they could have come right in front of some of the Negro places. But as always the Negro was wrong what Julian didn't understand that these farms to market roads were just out of bounds for the poor old Negro. But Julian didn't want to except that, Julian went onto say one time in church and the writer will quote him 'we colored folks want the same things the white folks want' We colored folks believe the same way white folks believe, we colored folks hurt the same way white folks hurt. We colored folk want the same opportunity as the white folks." Are we colored folks wrong for wanting? Then he would go onto pray, to god for enlightenment and deliverance? After the farm to market roads was put in place the government came up with another program that was a grant, building diaries and stocking the herds, man Julian was by first in line for that program. To Julian it seemed like it was god sent Julian qualified for a dairy plus twenty five head of jerseys cows The farm bureau office told Julian once he was qualified to go home and the Texas farm bureau would send him out a letter stating when he was schedule to get his cows and the milk barn to be built. Man this Julian was all happy and was jubilated.

Man he was going around making plan where his dairy barn was going to be built. Julian had forgot he was colored, because Julian looked in the mirror every morning he looked the same as the other white folks down here in Fannin County. He even had blue eyes and blond hair, he even had a daughter his only daughter she had brown hair, with a blond stripe down the middle. People who didn't know her thought it was a hair tint it wasn't it came straight out of her genetic pool the poor old Negro would say it was god sent Julian had also forget that he knew this white man, who had fifty acre of land also, he also had fifty acre of cotton allotment. The allotment was suppose to be base on how much land one owned, Julian could not figure it out since each owned fifty acres of land. The colored man got two acres of cotton the white man received fifty acres of cotton. Were justice serve here? Julian had forgotten because he believed in a super power so one day Julian received the letter he was looking for and he was jubilated. The letter was from the Texas farm bureau, Julian could not wait to open it, and he live about two and a half miles from the mail box. He ran almost every step of the way home from the mail box he didn't open the letter, because he wanted to share this special occasion with his wife Josie. Julian proceeded to open the letter and gave the letter to his wife Josie since she was the best reader. She proceeded to read the letter, the letter was in details explaining how he was awarded a dairy building and twenty five milk cows and one bull, but due to the fact that he didn't live on a paved farm to market road they the Texas farm bureau could not deliver as promise. The letter would on to say one must understand if it rained and the truck was coming to pick up the milk the truck could not get to your place, because you do not live on a farm to market road. Due to that fact, your claim have been rejected let us know within a year if you move to a farm to market road we will gladly review your claim Texas farm bureau. . Julian and Josie were jubilated when they received the letter but once they read the letter their jubilation turned into tears and Julian was never the same. Julian was the writer's father the writer is writing from experience, that letter from the Texas farm bureau not only poisons the spirit of Julian but also the writer.

So as on can see the system in which we live in, in this here America has a way of forming a complex whole. Not only damaging one but also damaging future generation of one. One may say that the system dams the soul of one and curse the future generations yet to arrive that is the power of the system that we live in, in this here America, we the typical American Negro.

The picture above is Denise and Coach J.R. DeHorney as children they were inseparable. They both are the results of the fruits of Slavery; they had no input on their soul, their soul derived from the results of yesterday. They grew up as friends both chose to depart as individuals as they grew older, but both, are sill connected by the reality of genetics. One chose to become a parent at 14, one chose to gain two degrees, both have the genetics of abandonment in their genetic pool. As a result of their genetic pool they have something in common they both abandon their children, a decision that derived from their choice. A choice that derive from their developmental behavior, a behavior that derived from their soul. A soul that derive from the fruits of Slavery a soul that was not program with love and understanding.

Mr. Walter Briggs who had a 2nd grade education said it best, when you find a child with a developmental problem follow that child home and when the parents answer the door you will find where the problem derived from.

In essence, what he was saying, follow the root system to the original, as you can see from the picture the roots would go directly too the master. Nobody knows the master better than the Slave or vice -- versa.

To sum it all up, the father and mother should bless their children not curse them; 'please' stop the cycle that started with the creation of the Typical American Negro.

CHAPTER 10

NO GOD
NO LOVE
WHY?

IN ALL FAIRNESS TO TRUTH Slavery ended in 1865, but in actuality the American Negro mind still exists in Slavery. As the poor old Negro would say Rome was not built in a day, the same with the mind the same with Slavery, the same with liberation that's the laws of nature. Since the poor old Negro was set apart for the appropriate use for white America. What Josie and Julian experienced that was some of the specifics that derive from that appropriate exclusive. So as the poor old Negro would say, one have to take the bitter with the sweet, and gain knowledge from that experience. And take that experienced and pass it on to the next generation that is called wisdom, this is what has happen in the past. This should preside on into the future, for example, history has taught us Uncle Ruben whom we the writer have talked about before in this book. When he was a Slave they the masters did not teach him about time, for instance the year, like the year was 1865, they would confused his mind they taught him about seasons. Like when a little Slave boy could wear short pants for 12 seasons, on his 13 season he would be considered grown and given a job. Plus he had to wear long pants, that's were time would stop for the Slave each Slave was appropriated for a specific job. This here uncle Ruben was appropriated to be used as a stud or one could just say a breeding machine in short a sex Slave uncle Ruben was told on his thirteen season he could no longer wear short pants or associate with his white brother since, he would become a man. He was told that he would work in the fields for five seasons at which time he would become a full time stud. Since he was going to grow up and become a very large specimen but, he uncle Ruben would have to serve his apprenticeship as a field hand to appreciate the value of being a super stud. Not only would he have the experience and knowledge of a field hand he would have paid a sacrifice for being a stud. Life is no different in the arena for other regimes, just what role did Christian religion play in it right or wrong? Here in this here America since the first ship load of Slaves arrived in this here America in October of 1562, remember the Africans were stripped of everything but ignorance and blackness. They had to let go of their religious beliefs before they entered the Slave ship history has already demonstrated that it was not until 1787 that the religion was given the okay to be taught to the Slaves. That was over 200 years my friends And this America was said to be founded on a Christian belief but the significance would be who's belief, history has plainly demonstrated that So the Slaves went without the significance of a religion for over two hundred years that is a life spans of 3, or 4 generations in the meantime, the Slaves were working seven days a week from sun-up to can't see building this here America. For what we know it as we write yes one can believe what they want but the facts remains the same that is the law of inheritance. In the meantime, the wild Africans that was brought to this here America was trying to be taught civilization. And the poor old Negro was being taught how to maintain what white America wanted for them other words, to be self contained from the first generation of Negroes. They were programmed to be teachers on how to maintain what white America wanted they the Negro passed that experience on down to the future generation of Slaves. Including the new arrivals from Africa, self containing is very important and still important as we write, that's why the ghetto's still exists as we write. One can just look at the ghetto and see where this here America wants the poor old Negro. So by being self contained no one would have to worry about the progress of the poor old Negro they are self contained, that's the typical Negro. Being a good American Negro is no different from being a good Christian both has to be taught, once you force feed the program into one it becomes innate automatic one has to understand the poor old Negro learned everything and I mean everything one could imagine from white America.

So how could any one in there wildest dream be oppressed for over four hundred years by a thing then go on their own then immediately know everything under the sun. Impossible under the sun we exists under, we the writer is still trying to figure out just what role did or how the Christian religion help build this here America? That's a very good question but at the same time, all one has to do is look at the facts and the facts' will just pour out on all open minded humans. And as we write there is no facts' to back up the fact's that the Christian religion played any positive thing in helping the Slave or the poor old Negro. The absolute facts do not point in that direction history has plainly demonstrated that. For instance, when the first ship load of slaves departed for this here America, on this ship called Jesus the owner of the ship was a highly religion man but yet and still he the owner and captain of this ship let the ship hands raped the wild African women he stood silent as if he or his Christian beliefs did not exists. And history says he not only stood idle before the ship docked at its American shores the captain and owner of this here ship Jesus. He also engaged in raping the wild African women.

The action of the Captain of this here ship Jesus, plainly demonstrated what he condone and condemned. As growing up in the segregated south the writer never heard of a white American clergyman saying anything against segregation that's an absolute fact. Now if the poor old Slaves go over 200 years, without religion just where can one say that this here Christian religion is for the poor Negro. It would be better to say that the Christian religion got lost, somewhere between prosperity and Slavery. One can very well see that, because history has proven that and history is your best teacher history only produces facts. By those facts, one can very well say that the original Christian religion played just as much a role as any in creating the dysfunctional Negro. With the facts that has been presented to the writer by history, the history that was left on a paper trail to provide to such people as the writer. One can only thank history for that One cannot not escape the facts of truth in order for fact to be pure one has to surrender to truth. The holy bible say the truth will set you free once, you are free, and one will be as the wind the wind blows freely just as truth speaks freely. Once one is free one will be speaking freely, of truth they no longer have to hide a truth. When one is hiding something it automatically point into the direction of falsehood, the same as Santa Claus the truth do not carry the effects of Santa Claus. If one follow truth one do not have to try and find the best solution to a stimulus just like pure water no one have to try to fix pure water. Pure means free from impurities, free from contamination meaning as the red man would say, free from a split tongue meaning one way. No one or no thing including the Christian religion can escape the law of purity when one is hiding and covering up and diluting purity one can very easily say that's ones emotion in transition. Think about the basketball players on how they make decisions in transition if, they make the right decision they will be rewarded. If they make the wrong decision it will be to know avail it will have the same value as the Christian religion had for the slaves from 1562, until 1787, there wasn't finer parable when Jesus said a tree is known for the fruit it bear. The poor old Negro would say that action speaks louder than words, the poor old Negro grew up with the motto saying when a person is hesitate in there thinking one can very well say they are thinking up a lie. If one is freely with there thinking that's means a decision is prepared from the facts. The facts the writer have presented to this point can one say that this here Christian religion that was brought to this America and helped lay the foundation for this here America as we know it as we write. Is it for the poor old Negro? Is it segregated? Is it for white America only? Facts will produce the truth, if one looks at actuality and not what one wants it to be or should be. Do not use the Santa Claus affects and expect truth for instance, if one says a fat white man comes down a chimney and go out the front door With a very clean red and white suit just where does the realization lie in truth or falsehood. You the reader be the judge from where facts lay this Christian religion that this American speak off only benefits a selected few that is facts pure and simple. One must remember, that the intellect takes advantage of the simple so, by the facts of history the poor old Negro did not benefit off of this here Christian religion until 1787, so says history when they gave the Slaves religious freedom they also stop the progress of working Slaves until they dropped . Meaning they stopped working seven days a week, meaning they had a day off but, work continued on Sunday now. Who do you think was cooking meals for master on Sunday? Who do you think was milking the cows on Sunday? 'yes 'you the reader are ever so right now let the writer ask you the reader a question When the poor old Negro begin there regime of Christianity Do you the reader think that the master offered them the same church service? As they the masters had? We the writer think not yes this Christianity were segregated the poor old Negro had to be programmed on how, and what to believe. The same with Santa Claus if the poor old Negro couldn't read how they could read for self all one has to do is think. One must remember that master controlled the plantation that including picking the Negroes preacher. From the writer standpoint, it is very plain and simple if one is building a structure that's going to be 12 stories high one must first build a foundation. From that foundation it will serve as base then, one proceeds on too build three stories then at that point the builder will decide to skip too the six floor now just what would the builder build on if he the builder decided to skip three floors. Just where would the support would be for floor six- thru twelve that's what puzzles the writer a structure is no stronger than its support and the Christian religion is no different. Now you the reader tell the writer Is this why the poor old Negro believes that nothing will turn into something? Is that why they taught the Negro about Santa Claus? One has a building twelve stories high and three stories of the building in the middle are missing or invisible, the laws of logics say that those three stories must be there in order to support the top floors so they must be very visible. Wouldn't you the reader agree? It's all about belief no actuality at all; if one can't physically build something that is invisible how can minds do the impossible, since the mind is what make the person.

What can one build on a belief, in actuality only another belief without actuality there's no facts to base a belief on? Just what is a base? A base is a place set aside too build a foundation without a base a structure cannot be built except, a structure of a belief one cannot win an argument with a believer. Hey just give it up. From the writer's experience if one find a believer that believer has always been in the forming position, to say it mildly it is only matter taking up space. The only significance of a belief is that of the believer in actuality, it has no significance to others. A belief only serve one in their emotional state of mind, a belief serves the same capacity as hope and a wish.

All three are in the same position, the position of which one function its there role in life it seems and it is very acceptable by the authorities. One must not forget the mind is what make the person, an individual is what they think and they are the ones who choose what to think and from that thought one develops a habit. And from that habit a character is born oh yes that character is inherited meaning it becomes part of their genetic pool the same as black and white no exception to the rule of genetics. One must remember a structure is no stronger than its support; one just can't build on a belief a belief is just that. Since we arc digging of into Christianity lets' dig a little deeper let the writer take you the reader into the dark blue waters of thought. History has said that the poor old Negro have went over 200 years without the Christian religion so, one can very well say without a doubt the poor old Negro have to taught the Christian religion. Now a question has arrived. Is the Christian religion a part of nature? We the writer will let you the reader decide for yourself and to your self can one say if one have to be taught something is that the beginning of a habit or a character. By the laws of nature if one has to be taught that is not nature that did not come from above let the writer explain about nature, nature is natural. Nature comes with the innateness of self; the reason the writer is putting this in because the writer was in a Church of god in Christ church in Phoenix AZ. On west Buckeye Rd. in a small church maybe about 40 people were in attendance. But first let the writer inform the reader on how and why this street is called Buckeye Rd. the road runs east and west. Back in the day when the poor old Negro was fleeing the south some American Negroes migrated to the west and south west, in Phoenix AZ. was no exception. The Negroes were coming to Arizona to pick cotton that was when cotton was king. It was said, by the way of hand –me –down information that it was so many illiterate Negroes coming to Phoenix AZ. They didn't know their place so they the authorities drew a map easily and understandable for the illiterate Negroes. Since the majority of these Negroes

Could not read or barley could read so the system name this road because Buckeye is one of the words that white America used in describing the American Negroes. They white America have been known to called the poor Negro buck eyed Nigger, so it seemed appropriate to called the road buckeye road. It would also, serve as a boundary line, no Negroes were allowed on the north side of Buckeye Rd. All Negroes were place on the south side of Buckeye Rd, so this church the writer attended was right on the South side of Buckeye Rd. The church was built in the thirty's during the migration of the Negroes. The preacher was about the same age as the writer, when the preacher gave his message in closing the preacher condemned nature lovers saying it was not part of god. Evidently he was not educated, by the proper authorities that reminds the writer, of a saying by the poor old Negro that preachers are like a travel agent they are always trying to send you to a place where they haven't been themselves. They are selling you a bill of goods about someone else's belief. The writer knew a gentleman from Ravenna Texas by the name of Manse Espy whom both of his grand parents was Slaves. Whom himself was born around 1898; he said a preacher was just a jack leg, saying the preacher was jack up with a bumper jack for the preacher could stand up. All one has to do as with any bumper jack is push it over and it will fall, if it is not blocked in. Meaning one cannot believe everything he says this preacher on Buckeye Rd, reminded the writer on what Manse Espy said. The preacher was unaware what nature was people must understand they are no stronger than their information, public speakers should understand that.

One should have facts to back them up, that is the Santa Claus affect it's alive and well as we write. Now let get back to the point were we were digging in this Christian religion it has been established by history. The same history established by white America, the same white America that was the owner of the Negro and creator of the Negro, the Negro could not read or write. Back in the 1500's that was the norm for the poor old Negro but, the Negro went over 200 years without any kind of Christianity. And almost 350 years without education so, how many generations did they go without a religion? That would be at least three or four generations it all depends on their life span, now once white America started teaching the American Negro the religion. Who appointed the teachers? Now the American Negro was taught to be self contained, when white America started teaching the American Negro the Christian religion they had to be taught it was not innate. It was not part of their inheritance meaning is was not part of nature, when one thinks of nature one would think of what nature has instill in a human without the aid of programming. It would be part of a human at birth for instance, discharging of human waste, breathing, swallowing, coughing, and sneezing would just be a small portion of what nature has delivered. When a baby is first born, their first breathe is on their own that first breathe ends with a cry or start with a cry now that's nature at its best unlike, the Christian religion where if one is not taught the Christian religion one don't miss it. How can one miss something they never had? As the writer grandmother Polly Topp would say, put that in your pipe and smoke it. The writer must remind the reader, that this here Christian religion had to be taught the same as cooking. Those wild Africans that were running around naked in their native land, as a nomad. Do you the reader in your wildest dreams think that the nomad African was running around naked with cooking utensils hanging from their side? We think not, where ever they were they were at home they had to be taught to just wear clothes, they had to taught to wear shoes, they had to be taught about personal hygiene. They had to be taught to cook their food, and foremost, they had to be taught this here Christian religion. Cooking utensils is not natural, in other words, one has to be taught this here civilization,

civilization is not part of nature one has to think, and one has to have an imagination. The writer want you the reader, to be on the same page with him in other word, the writer think that the holy bible says in all your doing get an understanding. So if white America, had something special they had to teach the poor old Negro for instance, the Christian religion. It was not automatic in all fairness it was not part of nature, can one imagine that the Slave owner gotten all of his Slaves altogether and started to teach them about their god how to be good. Can one imagine how the Slave owner went out and chose people to teach what he taught them the Slave owner? He taught them to be self contained that was the same scenario, when the wild African came to America wild and naked.

This reminds the writer, of a story that was handed down from Slavery the late Isabella Briggs- Harrington the co- author's first cousin who was born in 1895, and died at the ripe old age of 101 told the writer and his young son about a story that was very true. Ms. Harrington said she got the story from her grandmother; her grandmother was an ex- Slave and was in bondage somewhere around Pine Bluff Arkansas. While she was a Slave at this plantation, said that the master brought a African Slave to the plantation it was on a Saturday evening when this spectrum begin the master was driving the wagon he was bringing a new addition to the plantation the new arrival had a chain around his neck his hands were chain and the chains were chained to the back of the wagon. The Slave was trotting behind the wagon. He wore no shirt, he had no shoes on his feet, and his feet were bleeding very badly. All the Slaves gathered around, the master told us Negroes to get back this one are a very wild buck. I tried to put him into the wagon the master said but he didn't want to or didn't understand. He had shoes on his feet when I bought him he either pulled them off, or kicked them off he came all of the way from Louisiana like this. He had no shirt; this one is wild so stay, away from him he was very tall and black all the Negroes on this plantation were very light skin. So they took the African and put him in a shed, no bed, only some straw to lay on if he wanted too it was available to him. Ms. Harrington grandmother said that she remembers the master put a bucket of water into the shed with the Slave, and gave him a bowl of corn mush. They shut the door to the shed and locked it man you hear that African raising all sort of cane the master pick out a old man on the plantation his name was Tom Dooley all of the Negro called him Dooley but the master called him Tom. He was the only Slave on the plantation who had two names; I guessed one could safely say that he was the senior Slave. He was a very old fellow he was the preacher and he was the Negro who cut all of the Negro men hair. He was always telling the Negroes how to be a good Nigger. His cabin was close to the shed where the African was put, the master told Tom said Tom he had his hands full with this buck, but you have the wisdom to teach this buck a lot may god bless you with him and old Tom just said yes sir master. Because this Tom Dooley had been here before, the master would buy Slaves and bring them in for Mr. Dooley could program them on how to be a good Slave. This was Mr. Dooley job he was very good at that, to shorten the story —up for you the reader this African didn't want to wear clothes it was said that sometimes he would go for days and keep his clothes on. Then, all of a sudden you could open the building and he would be standing there still in chains all naked. They fed him in a trough like any hog he would eat with his hands it was said he acted well sometime then again, when Tom put the bucket of water in the building sometimes he would pick it up and throw it at Tom. Tom was a very small man all of the civilized Slaves were afraid of this African including Tom. Tom said he done all he could and Tom said he prayed day and night for the African he asked the master for some prayers to pray and he asked master to pray for him that was in the spring when they brought the African and the master was planning on having him ready by fall but it didn't work out that way. Ms. Harrington said her grandmother, said the master said we are going to have to get rid of him before thanksgiving. Because the master was afraid of him, the master didn't believe in whipping Slaves but it had been known the master let other Slaves whipped Slaves but not with this African. He was one of a kind. He never was unshackling from his chains while on this plantation, he left the same way he came no shoes, and no shirt. Still chained and trotting behind the wagon all of the

Slaves on the Plantation gathered around to wish him well. That was the only time, in which the African acted like he was part human a small grin appeared on his face when he left as if it was a relief. The other Slaves talked talk about him for the duration of Slavery it was a mystery and still a mystery as we write.

Was the African acting or was that his mental acceptance? I guess one will never know because that African was never seen or heard from since so, one can wonder or guess the African is the only person with the answer. Was he an actor or a man with a mental condition? When and what so- ever, one can believe what they want but the facts remains the same, when a person is wild they act accordingly. When a person don't know they act accordingly history has told us that on the end of Slavery down in Louisiana that some of the Slaves was so white they looked white. In actuality, they were white the only way in which one could distinguish whether one was a Slave or not were by their vocabulary. One may think that it is where the parable derive from that a educated person can act ignorant but, an ignorant person can't act educated.

The above picture is the new farmers of America chapter at Washington high school at Bonham Texas the Year 1960.

This picture is probably the only existing picture, the writer is included. The picture, describe each one as an individual meaning there is twenty -six different principles since the Negro is created to be an individual. Where there is no unity there is no existence for strength, or love, history has demonstrated that with the creation of the poor old Negro. Because of the root system all of the children in the picture went their separate ways some finished college - some didn't some went on the gain their PhD. it all derived from their root system. One has to remember it's all what one believe the mind is what make the person. But for sure all twenty - six have one thing in common, they were all created to be a endowment for America that's the typical American Negro.

Oh yea' the white man in the picture, is not white he is black, Yea 'right' it's your perception of belief, that's the typical American Negro. The typical American Negro is program what to believe but the facts remain the same.

CHAPTER 11

MR. CHARLEY HILL'S GRANDFATHER [1849-1956]

NOW DO YOU THE READER think that when the first load of Slaves arrived from Africa on this ship Jesus that this here America had houses waiting on them to live in? What the writer was told by hand me down and other ex –Slaves yes the writer knew an ex-Slave His name was Charlie Spence he was born a Slave in 1849, and he died in 1956 yes that would make him one hundred and seven the writer remember seeing him many times starting in 1950.

In 1950 he was a hundred and one he rode an old white horse, the horse looked as old as he was Yes he was 106 or 107 when he died he didn't really know one has to understand the Negro, was and is on a journey to information yes the poor old Negro has to learn how to exists in this here white America. The journey still exists as we write. So this here Mr. Charlie Spence was no exception to the system that white America put in position to rule. Learning is a slow process experience is your best teacher, Mr. Charlie Spence was told the Year he was born but not the month, and he was a full grown man before he learned the twelve months of a year. That's the reality of a system that do not exist for one.

As the poor old Negro would say, one has to find it as it is and move forward.

The poor old Negro would also say that life is a journey with each step it is a new beginning and a new experience and one can only take life a step at a time.

This here Mr. Charlie was no exception. The last time the writer, saw this Mr. Charlie was in 1956, just before he died as the writer said before the writer father was a Country preacher and Mr. Charlie Spence stayed about two miles by road from the writer if one would cut through the woods it was less than half a mile. If it was not for the woods one could see his house very easily when and what –so –ever the last time the writer saw this here Mr. Spence he was in bed. He was talking about what he knew all so well Slavery, Mr. Spence looked at the writer and told the writer to obey and cherish his mother Mr. Spence said he left his mother at 8 or 9 he don't know for sure which one because at the time he was just learning to count those numbers. Mr. Spence said it was very hard to learn how to count because he couldn't see what he was counting. Mr. Spence said he could count numbers but he couldn't write numbers he just had to use his mind no opportunities for this here Mr. Spence to go to school he was a Slave. His sole purpose was to obey, serve, and perform so his opportunity lay at the exposure of others. Mr. Spence would go on to say, that an older Slave taught him the year he was born so it would be a good guess that he didn't know the importance of the month. Mr. Spence said the older Slave knew the year because Mr. Spence was born about the same time as the older Slave came to the plantation the older Slave told Mr. Spence that he over heard the master saying that 1849, was a good Year and that 1850, was hoping to be a better Year from that the older Slave knew the year was 1849, the older Slave was taught bits and pieces about counting. So he passed it on down by what he knew, he told this here Mr. Charlie Spence that it was Negroes who could read Mr. Spence asked him what was reading Mr. Spence said The Older Slave just said it was stuff on a paper. Mr. Spence would go on to say that he was 8 or 9 when master took him and his older brother to a auction to be sold his older brother was name Fountain he was about 4 or 5 Years older than Mr. Charlie Spence It was very early one morning Mr. Spence said when master came in and got him and his brother. He knew something was very wrong on how his mother was crying she kept pleading with master she was saying no please master don't take my children. Then, she fail on her knees and where praying to the Lord boy I never heard a prayer like she prayed, she was begging the Lord like something merciful. The master told Fountain and me to put our clothes on and go and get in the wagon. We were taught to obey Master as if he was god himself, we went on and got into the wagon as master ordered, my mother was a very small little woman. She was running behind the wagon as master took off, and she ran until she couldn't, then she fail to the ground in the road. The few other Slaves gathered around her. On the way to the Slave auction, the master apologized in his way saying I didn't want to break you all up but you all can't do the work of a man. And I need a man on the plantation to work you eat like a man but you don't work like a man I told your mother that you all had to work more and I knew from that we where never coming back. So, when we got to the auction they sold us as a pair, Mr. Spence said he didn't remember much about the auction the only thing he remembered as the auctioneer made a speech before the bidding started. He said that we would be good for someone who were starting a plantation, that we could growth with the plantation that we would growth up to make a fine buck. Mr. Spence said he didn't know what a buck was, he would go on to say that he was well over a hundred and he remembered like it was yesterday on how is mother was crying . In actuality, he never had gotten over it; by now I guess I never will I always wondered why the lord didn't help her. I was always taught that the Lord would always be there for you but what happen when my mother called him I guess I will never find out. The writer's father the Country preacher tried to explain this to Mr. Spence why the lord didn't answer her prayer immediately after the writer's father brief him on his belief Mr. Spence looked real sad, and said to the writer's father preacher I still don't understand I guess I never will. The writer remembers the writer's father saying may god bless him and may god take his soul he died the following morning. But he left a lifetime of memories the writer remembers all so well on how Mr. Spence would be riding this old white horse. The horse was so old it had turned grey; with each step the horse took it seemed to be his last. The writer remember his father once said when Mr. Spence was riding that old grey horse by their house you know the writer's father said animal are just like people you take that old grey horse Mr. Charlie Spence is riding he is just like a Nigger he is on his last leg, but he is still trying to serve master the horse died about two weeks after Mr. Spence died as a boy the writer wonders did the horse die from a broken heart or old age or could one just wonder was it a combination of both. One will never know the answer; one could only speculate it was the drift of destiny.

Here are some of the memories Mr. Charlie Spence left behind and the writer want to share them with you the reader.

Mr. Spence would ride that old white horse by the house two or three times a week, he would have a store bought saddle on it. It was old it was so old it looked like it may have come from general Custer, sometimes he would ride right up past the house and would shout how y'all doing? And he would keep on going then, sometimes as the writer's mother would say uncle Charlie Spence is on a Spence fit because, he would look up and see us outside he would get off his horse and start whipping the horse for no reason he would whip the horse past our house and would not speak. Once past the house he would climb back on the horse as if nothing had happen, and continue on his journey. The horse would be walking with his head down just about parallel to the ground. Mr. Spence would have his head down while riding upon the horse. Mr. Spence would be riding as if he was tired or asleep, one could easily see that the horse and Mr. Spence were very compatible, too each other. When the horse died the writer remembers it as if was yesterday they drug the horse to near the property line which was adjoining the writer's property. That was about half way between the writer's house and Mr. Spence house the writer remembers going in the direction of the dead horse playing one day the writer went over there to look at the horse and to the writer's surprise a opossum came out of the horse in fact it was four opossums came out of the rear end of the horse. Right under the horse's tail, the writer thought to himself how people can eat opossums, the writer's mother told him stories about how people would cook opossum including herself. Mr. Charlie Spence was never seen setting in church on any row in the church accept the last row, whether the church was full or not. The writer remember the writer's father would tell Mr. Spence to come up closer to the front Mr. Spence would reply, no thank you I set here. Mr. Spence would reply if asked why he would set on the back row he would say he had problems trusting that god the white folks gave us. Because that god did his mother wrong and he would say that's the only thing I know about that god I just don't know. The writer do not know if this Mr. Charlie Spence was ever was baptized because if he was this is the way it was done back in the day. The preacher would take the new members who had not been baptized too a pool of water, the pool would be that of stagnated water. The pool or pond would be owned by the white man Negroes didn't own a pond that were deep enough for a baptizing. The creeks that the Negroes own were not deep enough; the pond the writer's father used was about 4 to 5 ft. deep and was owned by a wealthy white fellow who was a cattle rancher and a land entrepreneur. He was so powerful when Negroes left their his land he would just fence it in no one ever said a word. The old Negro school who's land that was a joining his when the school closed up he just fenced the land in, the school building itself, he moved the building about a half of a mile from its original site right on the lake were the writers' father used the lake for the church's baptizing ceremonies. The original school was put there about 1890, the first school of any kind for Negroes, in Ravenna Texas, it closed down in 1950, that's 60 years my friends it has a lot of history. By rights the land site and building should be a historical site but instead, its sets on this private lake as we write only in America that shows the power and guts that exists in the position of this here system that we exist under. Negroes talks about it just like the old Negro school in Ravenna but all Negroes have the same root system that Mr. Charlie Spence had and that original root system goes all the way back to 1562, on that ship Jesus yes it hereditary and a descendent of the typical Negro.

Mr. Charlie was the first Negro in Fannin County to own an automobile, it was about 1920, and Mr. Charlie Spence was the first too own any farm riding equipment.

Mr. Charlie Spence said that he came somewhere from Louisiana he didn't know where and he didn't know his father. He and his brother was sold too a young white man he remembers traveling two days before reaching Ravenna. When he got to Ravenna he was put in a supply shed the Negro called it a smoke house. In actuality, it wasn't a smoke house. A smokehouse is where one smoke meat but, the Negro call it smoke house in actuality the Negro didn't know what it was. The poor old Negro would just gave it a name if you would asked the Negro or tell the Negro the correct terminology the Negro would just say it almost a smokehouse. But, one just don't smoke the meat there that's the typical American Negro. Mr. Spence said that he and fountain spent the duration of Slavery in that little shed sleeping on a straw mattress, living with spiders, all kinds of bugs and rats and snakes. Mr. Spence said he remembers when he was told that Slavery was over; he didn't know what it really meant until he got hungry. He was sixteen years old when he was freed. He was happy just to be foot loose, and he never did try to run away because what he describe any white man was a Slave patrol. They gave a bounty for run away Niggers in Fannin County so why run away and you didn't know where you going. He and his brother were the only Slaves on this small farm. He and his brother did what he called the Nigger work mostly clearing land of trees and brush. They milk the cows, and fed the hogs, chop the weeds, gathered the crops and draw all the water from the well. Please don't forget cutting all the wood for heat and cooking. Upon being set loose as a free so- called Negro it was white people going around taking what they called census they wanted to know your name and Most Slaves didn't have a last name Mr. Spence was no different so when the white folks who was registering the Negroes told the Negroes they could give them the master's last name or just give them a name. Mr. Spence brother used the master's last name so his name became Fountain Oliphant so when the white folks asked Mr. Spence did he want to use the same last name Mr. Spence replied hell no, I don't want nothing to do with those people I am finish with Slavery. The white man who was registering the Negroes got angry and said what in the hell I am I supposed to put down? Mr. Spence replied Charlie Spence the white fellow wrote down Charlie Spence on a piece of paper and gave it to Mr. Spence that would be what was use for his name. It lasted a long time until some of his children saw someone with the name Spencer and they told him them that's how you suppose to spell your name. That's the way the poor old Negro did it and still doing it as we write that's the fruits of not knowing where one comes from something sound better to one then one follow. The poor old Negro have gotten good at that experience, history has plainly demonstrated that with the different names the Negro have used or been called. For instance, Mullato Quad, colored, yellow Nigger, African American, Afro American, coon, buckeye, spade, darkie, black, Sambo blackie, black nigger, black and lord only knows what else. One can only imagine what will be next, that is the results of not knowing and the response of a follower. When Mr. Charlie Spence died they wrote on his grave stone Charlie Spencer they took his rights of calling him what he wanted to be called Charlie Spence. Not all ex- Slaves had the opportunity to choose their last name the writer's great grandmother didn't have that opportunity that opportunity none existed. Just as new found freedom for the Slaves they quickly learned that freedom have boundary just as the writer's great – grand – mother experienced. Her master and the father of her oldest son, experience when she was set free. Her master name was Ebenezer Lafayette Dohoney but when he released her he gave her a note that stated her name since she could not read. He told her this is your last name Dehoney but that last name got diluted many times before it become settle with DeHorney by birth right the name should be Dohoney Mr. Spence could not read or look at numbers and tell you what they were although somehow he could count in all fairness he was against education saying education was only a tool for the white man. Only a tool, to make the Nigger a better Nigger for the white folks for instance, he would say if one can read and write they would send you off too war and die. For a war you know not why you are fighting only what you are told, you will be a Nigger either way. Growing up in the south it was some Negroes who just didn't want to learn to read and write. The writer run into quite a few probably about 30-40% in the Negro school Some would plainly tell you others would lie about it Some children would just say I do not need too read and write because I got a job when I turn sixteen. I am going to work for Mr. so- and so and when working for him you don't have to read and write, the writer heard that many times the writer himself didn't put emphasis on learning to read and write. When the writer was growing up his original plans was to be a truck driver. Then, he found out that a truck driver had to know how to read and write then, he switch to a mortician. Then once he learned that a mortician needed to know how to read and write he switch to a farm tractor driver. Then, the writer moved to Arizona he learned that they didn't let Negroes drive farm tractors in Arizona, or it was so hard to get a job as a tractor driver as a Negro it was as though it didn't exists so by now the writer was seventeen and had missed the basic of learning to read so the writer was caught between a limbo a rock and a hard place. Or in actuality, caught between discrimination and ignorance, from experience that's the pits of hell that is your typical American Negro that exist in this here America. So the writer can relate to the way Mr. Charlie Spence saw it may peace be upon his soul. In essence, what Mr. Spence was saying by learning to read and write the poor old negro was just preparing themselves to be a better mortar for white America better or worse the poor old Negro was created to obey, serve, and perform that's the typical Negro. Now just what is a mortar? Yes you the reader are ever so right history has plainly demonstrated that the poor old Negro are willing and game to give their live for the cause whatever America want the cause to be. The poor old Negro has provided their life as a service to this America. One can look at a poor old Negro all humped over laughing when its not funny, scratching when they are not itching, all old and still pushing a broom and trying to clean up America mess.

One can called that poor old Negro a mortar because they had given all they could unlike Mr. Charlie Spence he was 100 years old when he farmed his last crop with 3 mules. Why? Because he wanted to survived, he was not getting one red cent from social security. He had too obey Mr. Lincoln who told the poor old Negro root hog or die. Mr. Spence rooted for 100 years then lived off his daughter another 4 years before he was allowed to receive an old age pension in around 1952, that when it became available for the poor old NEGRO in Fannin County TX. Now wouldn't you the reader describe that person as a mortar to better this here America that's the typical America Negro?

Oh yes MR. Charlie Spence was the first Negro in Ravenna to buy a car yes it was a 1924, Chevrolet brand new at the ripe old age of 75 Years old. If most people are still around at that age they are about ready to give it up. Mr. Spence would say hope is just around the corner, hey, that's the kind of fellow that the writer would want to follow if the writer was a follower. Mr. Spence was a fellow who paved a road in a wilderness and he was a leader. He had natural hard facts to back a reality up, not a belief here my brothers and sisters just plain and simple facts.

The picture above is that of Mr. Charley Hill and Heaston Gentry wearing glasses and the lady is Heaston wife name unknown. Heaston is standing outside and Mr. Hill is in the middle. Heaston is on the outside along with his wife. She is on the outside. Mr. Charley Hill and Heaston is the grandsons of Mr. Charley Spence at the time of the picture Mr. Hill was 93 years old, Heaston and Mr. Hill are first cousins. Their grandfather Mr. Charley Spence farmed his last crop at 100 thanks to the laws of America the poor old Negro do not have to work until they drop, thanks America.

CHAPTER #12

THE POWER OF IGNORANCE
ITS HEREDITY:

IT'S NO THEORY, HOW THE wild African arrived in this here America naked with cooking utensils hanging from their left side, toilet tissue and sanitary napkins hanging from their right side and a welcome committee waiting on their arrival. No clergyman was giving thanks for their arrival yes the poor old African had to leave not only their Gods their hopes and dreams was taken away never to be seen again. The poor old Negro have said many times, that the reason the Negro sleeps so much it is because their dreams are better than their actuality. Do you the reader in your wildest dreams really think a Negro dream of a life in the ghetto or hood? Do you the reader think a Negro have a dream of poverty? Do you the reader think the Negro have a dream of being a crack head? Or do you think the Negro have a dream of being incarcerated? Do you the reader really think that?

As we write America is # 19th in the world in education and number one in incarceration of people. Just where do you the reader think that figure comes from it came it by the way of experience, remember America is well experienced in punishment but will hold one back on education.

Mr. Charley Spence was a prime example yet and still, one of his great-grandson graduated from college with a PhD probably as we write he do not know the history of his great grandfather that's the typical American Negro. Why? Because America programmed the American

Negro in a way for the youth when they grew up they wouldn't have to refine the adults. The way a educated Negro looks at it is they will go out and capture the limits of someone else's idea logics however, at the same time they will not know the foundation their soul were built on. They are like a city without a base; they have the same idea logics of a man the writer whom he met in Arkansas. The poor old Negro was born and raised on this plantation, he and his wife had twelve children. But he could not remember all of their names or ages, but at the same time, he not only remember master children, grand children, and great -grand children. In fact he knew their age, occupation, and geo- graphic location. What set this man apart from a Negro person with a PhD? Only the piece of paper that the PhD was written on the mind is what make the person and the mind derives from the soul. So one can very well say, that America have provided the poor old Negro with ignorance, and brutality but turned their back on humanity man how the writer loves history, because history don't lie it just provide the facts. Just as when the African arrived they had no welcome committee providing them with a clergyman or a table set up with food silverware, plates, and a glass of tea no napkin no chair to set in

No food prepared, no tablecloth, no place to bath, and no bowl of honey and these were wild Africans. Now do you the reader really think that's what happen? Or do you think they were driven inside a building like any wild animal out of the wilderness and their food was poured in a trough and their water was in a large water trough for everyone to drink out of. The writer remembers himself when water was poured in what they called a water bucket, and everyone used the same dipper to dip out the water and drink it from the dipper. The writer remembers one time, that he and his father had walked about 10 miles and we stopped in on this Negro family and asked for some water. The lady brought us a bucket with a dipper in it, the writer's father poured the water out of the bucket and went to the well and draw up a fresh bucket of water but the dipper remained. The writer said to his father daddy can I have a glass, the writer father asked why? The writer replied those people don't look to clean they look like they have been eating opossum. The writer's father replied go ahead and get that dipper and drink the water and be thankful. The writer's father said he remembers when their was no dipper, Nigger would just drink out of the bucket be thankful for all things that's the typical America Negro. Now are you the reader still with the writer? If the answer is yes do you think the wild Africans had portable restroom waiting for them? Or do you think they were led into a holding pen, like any other cattle would be they would drop their waste where ever. One can believe what they want, but reality don't change a thing yes one will think that the American would want to keep the wild Africans in their same environment that they derive from wouldn't you the reader agree that's the very reason why they deprive the poor old Negro from education and opportunity to keep them close to the original and at the same time, they are programming them for the future. The poor old Negro would say, they are killing two birds with one stone, and while all of this is happening just where is the Christian religion my friends. Since this here America was founded on Christian religious principles well my friends one have to understand as we write the average American Negro do not know what principle means, that's the typical America Negro. They were programmed to obey not to chase down facts, which are why education was kept out of the hands of the poor old Negro. For Negroes could not think for self. Now is that part of nature?

Did the wild Africans get off of that ship Jesus asking for the restroom? Or was it just like the Christian religion they had to be taught, all one has to do is think. Just as one eat and drink water, they do not have to be programmed to dispose of their waste that's nature at its best Any living animal are programmed by nature to dispose of their waste that's nature if one has too be programmed that means that's not part of nature that would mean that is part of a civilization the same as any community or environment. Since civilization is just an advanced stage of development of humanity.

That's the very reason, that America turned their back on humanity because humanity was out of bounds for the poor old Negro. America wanted the poor old Negro to be at level one which means the original state of mind at their creation which means in essence, just too exists. That's the very reason why, when the poor old Negro Asked for an advancement White America rejected that advancement it were to keep them at present existence, since the mind is what make the person.

White America programmed the poor old Negro one must remember that when one programmed a thing, that one can control that thing the poor old Negro is no exception. One must remember and can't forget that the idea logics came from the so-called Christian religion with no exception. There wasn't a finer parable when Jesus said a tree is known for the fruit it bears. One can thank their creator for history, without history one cannot see facts for what they are without history there would be no bible. Without being able to read one couldn't read the bible for self so, in essence what the writer is saying if it wasn't for yesterday there would be no today one can thank history for that.

That's the law of purity, so therefore, by the laws of creation all so-called – Christian has to be taught otherwise, they would not spend the time teaching. It would be a natural thing just like eating no one has to teach a baby too dispose of their waste they dispose of their waste automatically at the beginning of life. My friends that is pure nature it cannot get any purer than that, that's natural that's from the original creator the one who created all animals. Animals were created in a self contained environment would it be safe to say that if one is taught a thing that it comes from the creator? Or does it come from man? We the writer will let you the reader decide for self but, if one believes in Santa –Claus one believes in magic its all about beliefs. But the writer can only guarantee that the facts will remain the same that's purity it can't get any finer. Would it be safe to say, if one is taught a thing it is not natural it is not part of nature the writer will let you the reader decide.

Over two hundred years since the first ship load of Africans, arrive in this here America on that ship Jesus white America Began to program the poor old Negro with the Christian religion. The American whites couldn't teach it to the African for one the African was wild. Can you the reader imagine trying to teach a wild buck deer to read that was your wild African? So if not how can one teach one a thing when they don't understand what one is saying. The African could not speak English white America could not speak their tongue sticking with facts how could it be. So do you the reader think that white America's clergyman started praying for the Africans? The writer think not but you the reader, can think for self once the Negro was created, after three or four generations the poor old Negro began to understand what was going on. .So therefore, they could progress they could move to another level or in Slave terms another shelf they could count maybe 1, 2, 3 they went in stages when they were teaching them. They were teaching them this American Christianity. At their present position, they were something with no existence meaning nothing. Meaning they had no emotional value white America had to give them a mental value what better way to programmed the mind than that with the Christian religion. That would give them a sense of meaning of purpose, by having this new found purpose white America was able to influence the mind and emotions so well that its still exists as we write. A job well done. Who do you the reader think chose the clergyman for the Slaves? Yes you are ever so right the master the master attended all services because the master wanted to see how the services was conducted. The master wanted to stay in control in other words, he wanted to know what was going on, and wanted to know every movement. The master didn't want the Negroes plotting against him because they were still in bondage and they were being taught this here Christian religion. Two hundred plus Years after they came over here on that ship Jesus after they started teaching the Christian religion they freed them in less than a hundred Years. Less than a hundred Years the poor old Negro could be said that they were self contained, meaning they could be let loose or go too another shelf. Meaning, they could live in a house by themselves without boundaries, white America would let the greenback serve as the boundaries. The poor old Negro would be censored by the dollar bill this was the new America, meaning the changing of the guard. The poor old Negro would not only be censored, but guarded by the dollar bill and ignorance no more Slaves patrol ignorance and the dollar bill would serve that duty.

The events of time was changing or was it the drift of destiny, the American white Christian religion programmed the poor old Negro to believe that god didn't know them that is why master chose the preacher. Now after freedom in 1865, god had enough confidence in them, now god would choose the preacher {now what a myth}.

By the facts that is presented this here scenario, lead one to believe and let the reader remember that we are dealing with the facts that are present. From that fact and that fact alone before 1865, the facts say that anyone who owned a Slave was god because, master was god sent. The writer's bloodline started here in America in 1723, from Scotland and Ireland descent, the writer is talking about the DeHorney side of the spectrum. DeHorney derived from DoHoney in 1723, which derive from Scotland as a prisoner with the orders never to return again. Six years later guess what; Dohoney was a master the owner of six Slaves in Virginia so says history, thanks to the paper trail. Do that make DoHoney god sent? Or do the position, give Dohoney the power to be master and from that power do that gives one the right to play god. Well my readers, from the facts that are present in this here America the answer would be yes. Due to that fact in 1865, the events of time changed now the poor old Negro had the blessing and power of freedom of speech and that includes saying they were god sent and each individual has the right and power to believe what they want but, the facts will remain the same, for all you none-educators that is called choice and from that choice and that choice alone one can decide for self to do what ever they want. But from that choice they can form a habit and from that habit that choice will become one's character and that character will be passed on down as an inheritance. Meaning it is hereditary need the writer say any more the writer rests his case the poor old Negro has a saying; there is no blinder a person than a person who refuse to see. Let the writer remind the reader that the writer is blind, Scientist did a study they took a five gallon bucket filled it half way with water and put a rat in it, shut the door to a dark room. The rat lasted three minutes until it gave up. They took the rat out, fed it and gave it a 24 hour rest put the rat back in the bucket still in the dark room left the door open from that door it was getting light from another room. The rat lasted 36 hours before it gave up that is more than 700 times longer, that is the power of light. So, one can very well say by turning the Negroes a loose to fend for self now one has the power for hope, even though hope is worthless. They the poor old Negro have the opportunity of hope that was something the Africans didn't have when they came to this here America by way of Slaves ships. And tied in position by chains, their off-breed now have been given the position of hope after 300 plus years they can put hope into their vocabulary. And from that they can say or do what ever and just hope someone believes it. When someone say they are god sent everyone has the same choice to asked what god are you talking about. Where did your god come from? The answer may or may not surprise one; just look at the fruit that person tree bears before one decide to follow. The writer thinks that's a good choice. When one talks about god what god are they talking about? Are they talking about nature's creation or are they talking about the poor old Negroes creator the white American or just master. The writer has already established here in this book that one will not or cannot be taught what's automatic for instance ignorance. All one has too do is keep one in darkness to be ignorant, everyone is born of ignorance so by keeping one in ignorance automatically binds one to ignorance. But, if one has excess to light now they have the opportunity to see for self.

The above picture on the left is Junion and Josie DeHorney the writer's mother and father. To the right is Lillian Spencer Junion nephew and Mr. Charley Spence grandson. As with any genetics the power lies in the source, if the source don't want it will not be automatic the source has to want to unite. The writer's father would say one can't love if one don't want too one can't learn if one don't want too.

The writer's father would go on to say 'can' whip old can't until it could, meaning the poor old Negro was whipped until they did want. Which became their innateness to please and serve, the mind is what make the person.

CHAPTER 13

THE POWER OF LIGHT PRODUCES QUALITY

A T THIS POINT IN THE book, the writer would like to take the opportunity to tell a story an all so true story.

On how the writer force fed his son education one must understand, that the writer was the 2nd generation out of Slavery. The light the poor old Negroes were given after being cut a loose from Slavery the light was very dim. And by the time the writer derives the light had not been turned up. One can only imagine what is to be blind but the writer can provide one with facts about been blind or being an ignorant Negro. They are just about equal darkness is darkness whether its sight or one mental conception. When growing up with parents of an education deficits one thinks that way. Since you are what you think one cannot be without arms and think like they have two arms that's a no-no one cannot take someone were they are not. The writer was taught to exists and survive and the writer must not forget that he was taught to believe. The writer will skip most of the details and get to the point, the first sixteen years of the writer life. The writer was program too scratch, hope, and believe. The writer was raised in the country and taught how to survive in the country after sixteen years in the country. After the writer was planning to make a life for himself in the country that rug was snatched out from under him and he move to Yuma Arizona. Which was a hard working farming community Its main resources was alfalfa, melons, lettuce, and cotton but instead the writer was given a broom and mop at the ripe old age of sixteen. Who stood

6'2 weighed a hundred and ninety pounds and was called fat by his surrounding family from that, one can tell the intellect of that family. The writer went out for the football team made 2nd team varsity, on a play –off team and played the first game. Which was the only 2nd or third game the writer had ever attended and had only seen maybe four or five games on TV the writer didn't know that it took eleven players to make a team that's how illiterate the writer was. That was the type of blessing he got from his immediate family one must remember the writer mother told him at the ripe age of sixteen after he had received his broom and mop to go out and make the best hand for those white folks you can. Because we have provided for you for sixteen years and its time you start helping us that's in essence, what Abe Lincoln told the poor old Negro when he said root hog or die. The writer always believe if one do the same thing one will get the same results so the writer believed in change so when the writer son arrive he empowered a curse upon his son not to be like the writer or anyone in the writer's family. The writer's son had to be different and the writer would do anything to make it so, from the first day of school that's where the hard work began. Because the writer believed if one could train a show animal to compete in the county fair one could train a child to compete in the education department. When the writer moved to Arizona from Ravenna Texas it was not only a community shock it was an environment shock the community in Ravenna Texas was stagnated with the fruits of Slavery. They were about two steps out of Slavery man the Negroes couldn't even go to the county fair because it was against the law{ segregated} but in Yuma Arizona, these Negroes was training animals to be part of the county fair. It seems as if the writer's mother and father didn't want the writer to be part of that, that's why they gave me the broom and mop. The writer's brothers and sister seemed to be an agreement since the number two brother was the one who got the job for the writer. It was if they wanted the writer too experience the same thing they had the writer is talking about ignorance that is because the writer number two brother went to the army at sixteen. The writer's sister didn't work, until she finish high school but the writer knew none of his life is what he wanted for his son so the long journey too education began. Everything the writer did in his quest for excellent was wrong in the eyes of his people, they would tell my son things, like your daddy and mother do not know what they are doing. What 99.9% of the people don't understand, is that each person is born an individual first and foremost. What most people are not able to adjust to is the difference between light and darkness but it is as simple as 1, 2, 3 is to the writer but as the beat goes on it seems the majority of the people are not simple enough to adjust to the simplest as 1, 2, 3 that is the very reason the intellect takes advantage of the simple. In actuality, the poor old Negro would say it boil down to ignorance. The writer himself evaluated at an early age the fruits of other people the writer was very sensitive about this material. Since life is like a tree the writer look at each individual as a tree especially, what type of fruit that tree bear? For instance, if that tree was a none bearing tree the writer wanted no part of it for instance, if a person smoked they smell like smoke, and their breath stunk. So if the writer could smell that himself why would he do the same, he knew at an early age if he the writer did the same thing he would get the same result. So the writer didn't smoke because he wanted no part of smoking, the same with a broom and mop, there wasn't any prestige behind it. The writer looked at facts for instance, the writer looked at white America and how they got to where they are at as we write. Results did not come from obedience's then, on the other side of the spectrum the poor old Negro its seemed they were given a broom and mop for their obedience the writer wanted no part of it. Not for him, his wife, or any of his children he wanted the same as the richest white American and he used the same formula as white America, the results speaks for self.

Preparation speaks louder than words from mouth for example, the writer's son was potty train at nine months old weaned of a bottle at twelve months compare this to the writer's siblings children the writer's niece was still wearing diapers at two years old and weaned from the bottle at four years old. This was the number two brother daughter but, this was the gage that was used to compare the writer with the writer's people never asked what results the writer wanted they just told the writer what it was going to be and tried their very best to make it happen. But as we write and as we said before, the writer used the formula that white America used and one can very well say, the writer got a favorable result. The writer got that result, from his own idea logics and not by following some other simple individual. As a matter of pure facts, the writer have receive more sound advice from the so- called- no- body than he has from the preachers of American excluding the writer's father may peace be upon his soul. For instance, the Negroes of Yuma, Arizona the poor old Negro didn't have a country club or a boys club so what was considered the lower class of Negroes would gather in a vacant lot across the street from a liquor store on the corner of third street and fifteen avenue that was their corner all day and part of the night. They could be seen drinking their wine and beer, at the age of about eighteen the writer started visiting the corner although not indulging in the activity of drinking the writer just wanted to be part of the scene. With nothing else to do it seems that was the only thing that existed for the Negro in this here Yuma the writer was looking out of a very narrow scope. Then, one day one of the veteran drinkers of that corner the writer don't know his first name but his last name was Mr. Bohannon and he asked writer what are you doing here? The writer replied were are just visiting Mr. Bohannon replied you just look around and see which one of these wine O's you one to be like and pick that person out. The writer looked around and their were about twenty Negroes there drinking all drunk or about drunk. Mr. Bohannon would go on to say you are a very clean young man you remind me of myself, when I was about your age. I started young clean and fresh nothing has any exception, because something can turn into nothing but anything cannot turn into something you see my hand? The writer replied yes sir' Mr. Bohannon asked what do I have in my hand? The writer replied nothing; Mr. Bohannon reached out with his hand as if he was grabbing something then asked what do I have in my hand? The writer replied nothing Mr. Bohannon then replied well son, now you see nothing turns into nothing so there is nothing on this corner for you so you get the hell away from this corner and never return because there is nothing here for you. Mr. Bohannon asked do you see old Elmore over there? The writer replied yes sir, old Elmore was setting there all drunk and disoriented his wine bottle still in his hand slobbering from his mouth each eye looking in a different direction well, old Elmore has a mother and father at one time he was your age but no- one told him not to come to this corner because if they had Elmore may not be setting there now. Mr. Bohannon would go on to say that is your future if you continue to come. back Mr. Bohannon asked Elmore saying Elmore do you want an apple? Elmore replied is it organic? If it is yes if not no I have to watch what goes into my system said Elmore that was the summer of 62 the writer guess that Mr. Bohannon was about sixty at that time he was an older fellow. As the writer was leaving Mr. Bohannon got up and told the writer if you ever write a book say Mr. Bohannon never did advise you to be a drunk. Mr. Bohannon said he didn't want to be a wine –o but it was the circumstances saying the circumstances have beat me down now I am weak because I gave over to my feeling. What feel good is not always good so be strong and stay away from weak things and you will do alright in life that was the advice from what the community called a wine-o the writer calls him a true brother may peace be upon his soul. In essence what Mr. Bohannon was saying one can only say where life have led them, but they can't say where life will lead them the opposite of what the writer family tried to lead him too. The writer can say with all honesty the writer got to the position as he is as we write without the aid of the selfish. Thanks to people like Mr. Bohannon, the writer has learned from the best teacher on the universe that Mr. Experience, experience has taught the writer that the simple try to instill fear and doubt into one support. Support make the structure without the support of Mr. Bohannon the writer may not be writing this book as we write because doubt holds one back just as one, cannot go to Tuesday while holding on to Monday. One cannot hold on too ignorance while gaining success that would be like sneezing and chewing gum at the same time that is impossible as we write my friends. It seems very simple that the poor old Negro was program to do what feels good and natural they were not program to do what produces. It seems very simple that the poor old Negro would rather talked about a thing rather than have a thing. Could one say is that a Santa- Claw affect? So the writer is still trying to find out just where do or did the facts derive from for the preachers have for their parable that they are god sent because if one take out the belief one has nothing remember the demonstration Mr. Bohannon did was that facts or not. The writer is still talking about the typical Negro One must remember and cannot forget a structure is no stronger than its support.

So by the laws of nature, if one pull their support the structure will fall, the same with the so- called – wine-o if one pull the wine there is no more wine-o the same with ignorance if everyone strive for wisdom there would be no ignorance therefore, there will be no hump-back Nigger pushing a broom and pulling a mop and bucket with a vacuum cleaner strapped to his back. Proclaiming that he is gods gift of knowledge there were no finer parable when Jesus said a tree is none for the fruit it bears.

Just like every tree, it's supported by its support system one can very easily see that a tree is supported by its root system. The bigger the root system the better the support is for the tree, longer the root system the better for the tree that's very plain and simple. That's as simple as 1, 2-3 yet despite the simplicity of that fact enables the intellect to take advantage of the simple for instance, as we write there are Negroes who will argue that this here Christian religion was god sent. Despite the facts it is very simple if one pull the support of the structure there will be no structure the same if one eliminate ignorance from their equation don't one know there will be no ignorance. So by the laws of nature, even ignorance need a support base, history has plainly demonstrating that with the poor old Negro. The Negro was supported and still is supported as we write by their original biological father the American whites. That original trait, by the laws of inheritance still exists as we write. Why did white America keep education out of the hands of the Negro? Now that education is available to the poor old Negro why do that Negro still ignore education and cleave to Christian religion its very simple don't every child want to be acknowledge and excepted by their parents. Doesn't every parent want to be envied by the neighborhood hey 'man don't you see its just goes round and around where it stops no one knows that's the laws of inheritance? Scientist say that one drop of blood last forever in the genetic arena and forever is a very long time that is why one see a humpback Nigger pushing a broom at the age of 12 and continuing until they can't see preaching the same sermon because they are the star of darkness. Because they know for sure they have the support and backing of their biological father every child want to be the envy of their parents the poor old Negro is no exception. Experience do not mean nothing to the typical Negro, the typical Negro just want master to have his way so in essence, this hump-back Nigger, who gave all he had to the cause have the same equation of a Slave who worked from sun-up to can't see seven days a week and looked to master for guidance. This reminds the writer of a story that told to him by a little old lady she said she knew this Negro who was 6'6 and was a uncle Tom from his heart a hard working Tom. A Christian Tom, who did everything right he had so much knowledge that when he died he could not fit into the casket so what they did in order to bury him they gave him an enema and buried in him a shoe box. That's reminds the writer of that hump-back Nigger who idolizes himself that goes to explain what type of support one have will determine the structure. Oh' yes Jesus said it best when he said a tree is known for the fruit it bear each claim has to be backed up by a fact for instance, if one produce a claim to an insurance company it has to back- up by a fact if not it will be considered false, and is punishable by the law that is the law of the land. One should govern themselves accordingly doesn't one understand they need facts to convince a none believer a word is not a fact. One need an example to prove the facts of reality How can one believe that hump-back Nigger who is cleaving on to his broom and mop but explaining to you that he had the gift of knowledge that came from above. But all while that hump-back Nigger do not have enough faith in his own wisdom to turn that broom and mop a loose and use the wisdom from above that he is trying to convinced another with. Where does his belief lie? That reminds the writer of a story, that a preacher was preaching a sermon about faith and believing it was all about giving the preacher would go on to say it was a blessing to give. In fact the preacher said it is more blessing to give than to received all one has to do is pray then they would be bless the bottom line was asked and it will be given. When he got ready to leave he the preacher asked the congregation for money so he could buy gas to go home. This is a very true story the writer was a small boy in a country town the writer often asked himself as a child how could that be because the facts show the preacher didn't believe himself. He was trying to sell the audience a bill of goods that he wouldn't buy himself, he and the hump-back Nigger had the same equation it seems. Does one know that the logics will always lie within the claim? So its very plain and simple if one is god sent it will be very beautiful just like every creation think of the blue sky on a clear day. Think of the sun, think of all living plants, isn't that beautiful, that beauty has the material to back it up no belief system here, just absolute. When one has a paint brush one can paint any picture they want, history has plainly demonstrated that with the first ship load of Slaves that came to this here America. For all its worth, someone took a paint brush and painted Jesus on that ship but believe you me on the inside of that ship it was not Jesus, because we have been taught that Jesus is love. Would it be safe to say that the typical Negro suffer from a behavior disorder? The writer wonders because when the writer was growing up if the writer saw someone make a mistake he wouldn't do the same thing that person done the writer would try and change strategy. The writer would try to improve on a situation, for instance, some people go out and use drugs, drink the fire water go out and sale their bodies and end up on skid row then procreate children. The children grow up in that environment then; the parent talks about how successful their children are going to be when they grow up. Can't one see for self that if one do the same thing as some one else before them. Do they realize that they are going to get the same results? From that fact and that fact alone is that the reason the poor old Negro was here in this America for over 200 years without the aid of the Christian religion. Was it because that they had a behavior disorder or a developmental disorder? It has to be a reason doesn't you the readers agree, the writer is leaning in that direction? If one look at the facts as they are one will have to admit that white America is a progressive race of people sure they have a support group to support their structure, Although it seems the poor old Negro had more support when they were turn loose in 1865, than they do as we write. Why is this? Was it the association with master? Or was it the genetics being more pure then than it is as we write? Have the pureness of the Negro been diluted? And from that affect it has weaken let the writer look at some facts case and point in 1900, Negroes owned more property then they do now as we write. Negroes owned food, stores hardware stores, and restaurant; it seemed it was about having something for self. Negroes built their own house with their own hands, built their churches, and had pride in what they owned. They were proud of their net worth that was all in the past.

The picture above, is the co-author Louise standing with Shauck-daddy a registered Rottweiler whose' father was a trained working police dog and his mother was a show dog.

We illustrated this picture to illustrate, that all animals including humans have the same genetic innateness that derives from their genetic pool. The writer had very little training to do with Shauck, he was breed to serve and protect. He never tried to run away or leave his property if the gate was left open, he would just lay down at the entrance of the gate to protect from intruders.

Shauck loves to walk and he loves to show off, as little triple T' would say, he love to be the top dog. 'Yes' he's a dog but as any animal he knows how to use psychology, as we write he's ten Years old in human life. He no longer want to walk he tried to preserve his energy to protect, at night he's up and alert as long as he hear any gang members whistling, or prowling, at night Shauck is letting his presents be known.

Shauck has been a loyal servant all of his life Shauck reminds the writer of a good Nigger. The Negro was created with the system of Gothic love, any system have the innateness to form a complex whole on its environment that's why the poor old Negro was introduce to religion to maintain that Gothic environment. Education was out of bounds to the Slaves and when the poor old Negro was release from their chains that complex whole, that bounds still exists in their mind. The Negro had to fight for both, education and change. The Negro was not taught about the god of Eros' that God is love; love is and was out of bounds, to the mind of the poor old Negro. And once again, the mind is what make the person.

CHAPTER 14

THE CHANGE OF EVENTS

As we write, the poor old Negro is proud to have a high mortgage, high car payments, no insurance for the children and going to white America high dollar restaurants. Is this what integration done for the Negro? The writer remember when his late sister, graduated from high school back in 1954, in Yuma Arizona shortly after graduation the writer and his family move back to north Texas back to picking and chopping cotton. Back trying to make something out of nothing or can the writer just say we were hoping for a miracle that never came the writer sister moved back to Arizona in June of 1956. She obtained a Nigger job as a maid, the writer sister always looked after the writer. She was trying to give him a new identity; she would even fight for him. It were like the writer was important to her, it was like the writer's sister was the mother of wisdom. Man when she spoke the writer listen man the writer remember when his sister got the job at the motel she was so proud. She wrote and told the writer that she saw this real pretty jacket that she was going to buy for him. The writer wrote back asking her what kind of jacket was it; the writer's sister wrote back and said it was a suede jacket. The writer never heard of a suede jacket he asked around and no one ever heard of a suede jacket. So, the writer was very curious but when the writer received the jacket he found out quickly, that a suede jacket didn't belong in the country. Just wait for a rain, the writer didn't live on paved streets so when it rained that meant walking two mile to a bus stop every step of the way in the rain, and in the country that also meant mud. So if you wore a suede jacket that meant you would be soaked by the time the bus came that was the mentality of a country boy no exception to the rule not even the writer. The writer's sister would send him chomp change even after she got married in December of 1956; she still showed love for the writer. In the winter of 1960, the writer moved too Arizona, to the writer surprise a broom and a mop was awaiting the writer upon his arrival it was as if the writer had became a man. At the ripe old age of 16 it was a new beginning things was beginning to change between the writer and his sister. The writer's sister called it the changing of time, but the writer would like to express it was the events of time. The writer does not know where the fault lies, but the writer does know that the writer had obtained a different segment of people. He had an audience of follower in Texas; he played basketball as a freshman and sophomore on the junior varsity level. They didn't have a pair of shorts to fit him, even though he wore a size 32 that alienated the writer. When the writer tried to play football they didn't even have a helmet to fit him, the helmet was hand me down from white America. The helmet the writer tried to wear hurt his head, and it didn't fit. So that made the writer feel like he was some kind of freak in a freak show couldn't play football because no helmet was available. Had to play basketball in sweat pants but when the writer moved to Yuma it was a whole new ball game the writer lost two years in the transition. One can just say it was the fruits of ignorance need the writer say anymore about ignorance. But that ignorance experience still plagues the writer as we write, despite the obstacles the writer found the difference between the have and the have –knots... When the writer finally got to play basketball Yuma not only had a pair of pants to fit him they also had a warm- up suit and a bag to put them in. And all kind of support to support the players like the school newspaper, the town newspaper, a county newspaper and even a radio station played tribute to the team. Man this country boy who was use to waking up to milking cows and that was the last thing he did before going to bed, seven days a week come rain or shine. The writer was thankful for this new found glory. Not to mention the boxing career that the writer had the writer will not even talk about that but the writer do know for a fact with this new found glory it was the separation between him and his late sister. Was this the fruits of integration? Or was it the drift of destiny? I guess we will never know for sure the writer can remember his mother and father even the writer wife talked about how her mother and father would talk about the unity the poor old Negroes had in Arkansas. They would talk about neighbors building houses for neighbors, they would talk about the neighbors killing hogs and the whole community would have meat. They would talk about neighbors growing a garden and the whole community shared the garden. They would talk about the unity among neighbors not so as we write it seems after integration Negroes became more of an individual. Negroes wanted to be affiliated with white America it seems the poor old Negroes forget where they derive from. It was like the poor old Negro wanted to unite with white America and vanish from themselves. Was it that the typical Negro hates himself? Or is it the typical Negro cannot exist or don't want to exist as an individual. The writer remembers when he left the country in 1960, there about 40 families in this community, each family stayed about a mile apart. They had two churches and everyone worked in unison but, when the writer moved to Yuma if were about 40 Negro family stayed in a square block if was like a village. .It served as a base for a route to Los Angeles they called it Biggsville it was owned by an old Negro couple. It only had five houses including the owner house the rest was apartments some of the apartments didn't have a restroom just a place for a bed. They had what they called a community restroom; some where about a half of a block from their apartment but this were common practice on the west coast. Man it was all sorts of Negroes there it was farm hands, where house workers, cooks, maids, janitors, dead beats, wine-o, drunks, musicians, drug dealers, truck driver, and yes prostitute. Whatever one wanted they could find it over at Biggsville, they even had their own junk joint but they didn't have a store. But it was a Chinese store about a mile away yes they even had a disable vet. He became disable while serving in the military who didn't know that he was entitle to any army benefits. He found out about 30years later that he was entitle to a service connected injury, he found out from a Biggsville graduate yes it is a fact that two of these formal residence has graduated from college. That's the product of a typical Negro.

The laws of inheritance say that every procreation, would inherit the genes that was handed down now you the reader don't misunderstand the writer just because one is a drunk or drug addict that automatically produces the same that's not the case. History has demonstrated that with the poor old Negro, once a soul is damage, its means just that Say for instance, that a procreation comes from damage goods that means that their success and desires will be more of a possibility to be worsen than that of a none damage genetics pool. Meaning yes all damage goods can be repaired if one turn from their shadow a shadow is darkness otherwise, one cannot see it. A shadow is not invisible if one try to out run their shadow, they will live a life time and find out the facts that one cannot out run their shadow. So, in essence there is one more generation lost, but if one turn from their shadow it will began a new beginning. What the writer is saying to be brief is if one does the same thing that has damage their soul they will get the same result as the cause for their defect. So just where is the margin for improvement, so 'yes' my dear friends you the reader are ever so right, there is none and none is absolute nothing. Remember Mr. Bohannon prove that to the writer, that is the same scenario nothing is nothing wherever one places it. Now would that be the reason, white America didn't teach Christianity to their Slaves for over two hundred years because they didn't understand, because they were dysfunctional. The writer is leaning that way in his thinking more than ever since the experiments that the writer has done on the typical American Negro. One has to admit on the whole white America is a progressing people they didn't come to this here America naked without shoes on their feet they had clothes on. Someone had to teach the poor African, to put clothes on and by wearing shoes that would protect their feet. That would be the same as trying to teach a dysfunctional Negro that they need education for protection they just wouldn't understand the logics the writer has experience that first hand. When he was trying to learn to read and write his late fourth grade teacher Ms. Dorothy

Rayoback tried to explain the logics of protection but by then the writer had been program with the power of magic and it sounded better than the facts MS. Rayoback were delivering hey' that's the power of ignorance and Ignorance will always rule if one try to out run their shadow because all one has to do is say I don't believe. I still believe that nothing can turn into something all one has to do is ask a believer. And that believer will give one all the imaginary facts they want then, turn around and tell you, you have to believe that's the power of ignorance. In most cases, by the time one come to that conclusion there is another generation lost so just where is the margin for improvement. For a person with a self convicting mind when someone has convicted themselves it is impossible to unconvict them that's the power of the mind and the mind is what make the person. Just because white America is a progressing people that don't mean they are the most gifted people on the universe, because they went out and breeding with those naked Slaves. And if those Slaves were running wild and naked in Africa that meant that they were not running around with a role of toilet tissue in one hand and a sanitary napkin in the other hand. So, therefore by the facts of reality those Africans were not the cleanest people on the universe and by white America going out raping them and by that fact and that fact alone says that white America, have a behavior problem to put it mildly. In fact one can very easily say that they are a psycho. Now to you the reader, would you be proud of your children if they duplicated what the original founding fathers manifested. These facts came from history, the same history that say this here America was founded on the Christian religious principles. But what it didn't say was worse than what it said. You can believe what you want but the facts remains the same one has to explore all possibility to get to the facts so , from 1562, to 1787, one can very well say it took white America that long to instill the imaginary power of belief it's very hard to teach someone something they can't see. So in essence, what one is doing is teaching one the power that nothing is something in your wildest imagination can you really imagine what nothing is. How can one exists as something that is nothing 'hey' man one has to be on some powerful stuff to believe that but, that is exactly, what white America empowered the poor old Negro to believe. The poor old Negro will argue with someone who is trying to help them and will smile, at someone who is trying to hurt them. 'Hey' this is power at its best the writer's great grand father called it magnetic power the same power a snake have to charm and catch a bird. In other words, that person is powered by another spirit. That's why the typical Negro is so slow in progressing is because of their mind set, the writer has already demonstrated that with his experience, information come to enlightened one. The writer had the experience, of trying to help a seventeen year old girl with information about education and the girl frankly told him that she wanted to go out and experience things for her self. She didn't want a quick way to success to put it mildly within three years she have the experience of not having a high school degree or any college and for her labor she now has two kids, no father figure, and no job skills. Can one just say ignorance rules, or is it the drift of destiny, or can one just say the girl was using the information that she gained from nature and her personal progress one can only believe. One can only believe and the facts remains the same, the writer was program to believe that if he had it everyone else had it the writer was program to believe that. That is the very reason the writer didn't believe Ms. Rayoback because the writer was taught a different ball game but when he got to reality or to the game it was a whole new ball game, but the belief factor was still intact and the facts was on the other side of the spectrum. They were so far apart one couldn't unite them to get a positive results that my friends is the life of a typical Negro yarning for a place to belong. Back in the day, white America would say he is a good old boy, but as we write there is no demand for a good 'old boy' anymore.

The writer have experience just that, the writer is talking about behavior disorder for instance, when the writer was program for 16 years, to be one thing then, about the time he reached maturity the writer parents turn around and handed him a broom and mop. But they had convicted him to be a survival but, about the time the writer could utilize the talent that was presented to him the writer was given a new identity. What he had been taught now had become obsolete that is the typical Negro my friends if one don't know where they come from how can a person program a person to be at a scene of advancement. When the writer was growing up, he was taught by this here Christian religion that his mother and father so love the writer was taught is was okay not to read. Because if the lord wanted one to read and write the lord would teach you so the writer was taught it was against god will to play sports, or be a musician in a blues band. But it was okay to clean- up the arena after an event. That Christian religion still teaches the same as we write but it just a different event; the events have changed the teaching is the same. They teach one to have doubt, not knowing that doubt holds one back the writer was taught if the writer had it everyone else had it the writer was nothing special. The poor old Negro was taught to be self contained, even today that still exists by the fruits of Slavery if one doesn't turn from ignorance it will exist forever, and forever is a long time. If one goes back to ground zero and try to find the correct answer for why the Africans -was running around wild and naked in Africa. Why did a small minority of African suffer from that dilemma since Africa had a governing body but yet and still they had a behavior disorder despite what some arguments are about what type of Africans, came to this here America about King and queens coming to America? As always one can believe what they want but the facts remains the same if it was kings and queens that were rounded up in Africa they were strip of that title before entering the ship. By the time they arrived in this here America their titles had no value, the same value that the writer had when he was taught to survive in the country. But when he arrived in Arizona, that value had no value to a broom and mop see how history repeats itself. The majority of the poor Africans that was brought to this here America were not running around wild with cooking utensils in one hand and toilet tissue in the other hand. That did not exist because it is very dysfunctional Negroes right here in America as we write; there are Negroes that the writer knows off personally that don't have use for toilet tissue. The writer himself didn't use toilet tissue at home until November of 1960, when he moved to Yuma, Arizona What did he use? He used a corn cob or an old rag 'hey' the poor old Negro wrote the book on being green but they just didn't market it. now would you describe that person as having a behavior disorder? Do they know right from wrong? Some people, have to be caught, tied up, and drug to a scene before they will react to a stimuli like education; they had to be just literally made to improve. Its very sad but true their mind is resistance to growth, and the mind is what make the person. All of that have been demonstrated by history that is one of the main reasons why it was and is so easy to keep the Negro dysfunctional. Because they have not only been program to be dysfunctional but to obey by obeying, one will remain in their original state of mind unless, they are program to progress. Some poor old Negroes fight to stay in their original state of mind, even after Slavery it was said that some Negroes would argue that they were better off in Slavery. That would be the same as a baby would say that they are better of in diapers the poor old Negro was and almost is just like a baby. A baby will exists in diapers for just as long as one will put diapers on them. Some kids are potty trained at 9 months old and some children at 12 months old then, you see other children wearing diapers at 2 years old. The writer has experience at that, one of the writer's children was potty train at 9 months old thanks to the child mother thanks Louise for a job well done. The thanks comes from coach De Horney of Jack Yates high school Houston Texas, now on the other side of the spectrum, the writer niece was potty trained at 24 months old. Coach De Horney was weaned off the bottle at 12 months old the writer niece was 48 months old when she became weaned off the bottle its all in the mind set. The mind is what make the person, the poor old Negro have a saying when you find a fool use them that goes to explain why the intellect takes advantage of the simple. As white America would say if you find someone down keep them down because they may get up and do a reversal, history has plainly demonstrated that white America have the no how and power to keep one down as the poor old Negro would say believe you me. When and what so ever do you the reader know why the poor old Negro don't know their past, because they were not program to know their past they were program not to dwell on their past the past is gone forever. So say the poor old Negro that is water under the bridge, one can't pick up spill milk, that still exists as we write. That's' goes to explain why most Negroes can't talk about their great-grand parents because they know nothing about them. The poor old Negro has a saying, don't look back because your shadow may catch you and hold you back.

One has to look at truth as it is and the poor old Negroes problems is no exception, the Negro was program to serve and perform. And to serve and perform one can't worry about what happen to their mother, to be a good server or performer one has to worry only about the task at hand. Just like any good wine 'o one can't worry about yesterday wine heaven only knows where yesterdays wine lies. So, the wine o's only worries about consuming wine as of now yesterday will take care of self. The same with the Negroes Christian religion for instance, the poor old Negro do not think about what happen between 1562, and 1787 they would probably say why worry about something you can't change. Hey' we can do it today that's the very reason, the poor old Negro adjust so well they were program to be transition people. For instance, the writer is an good example, the writer was told don't worry about why you can't read if the good lord wanted you to read when he the good lord sees fit for you to read then, you will read. If the good lord don't see fit for you to read just be thankful, because the bible tells one to be thankful for all things, which includes not reading if one cannot read. That is a good example, why the events of the so-called Christian religion change so drastic, and have an everlasting affect on the mind set of a true believer. For instance, if the master pick out the preachers in one event and the next event god will choose the preachers. Couldn't one say, that's a traumatic event, but the poor old Negro have been programmed not to worry about yesterday as a result of that obedience the poor old Negro have been deprived of knowledge. Wouldn't that qualify one to be of darkness? One must remember that not knowing is the most dangerous spot on the universe one must understand in order to be a good people one must reverse the role. Turn that not knowing, into knowing then one will not have wine o, drugs addicts, and teenage pregnancies. That would no longer exist if one would surrender to knowledge of purity that would bring understanding and the love and pursuit of wisdom. Obedience must start with self; from that affect a rebirth of will, emotion, and a refined mind would serve the poor old Negro. Because by the law of knowledge and wisdom one can't do the same thing and get a different result, my friend's history has plainly demonstrated that with the poor old Negro. That's the typical American Negro still trying to explain how nothing can turn into something. Why does this still exists? Why? Because the poor old Negro have not gained knowledge from experience to conclude or come to the consumption the power of knowledge and by the laws that power is knowledge. One will derive of the affect of knowledge, to conclude that nothing is nothing and the power of a belief is not stronger than nothing. Nothing do not exist no belief will change that all one has to do is to take facts for an example. For instance the writer remembers when he was growing up as a uneducated dysfunctional child he was program to believe by this here Christian religion that is was against Gods will for a person to be an athlete. That was the event of the day when the writer was growing up. Now the event of today is that athletes were given that ability as a gift and it was god sent. Now isn't that confusing? Or contrary, to what the writer was program with that my friends show one the power of belief the power of belief can change without notice because the writer did not get the notice that the belief was changing. Now is that equal under the law, or is just plain ignorance. We the writer will let you the reader decide for self.

The scenario, the writer just tried to explain is the same as with the master choosing the preacher then with the changing of events god chooses the preachers. It all boils down to the belief just who or what is the key for the believer. The writer is not trying to persuade the reader in anyway, just putting the facts on the table, the same facts that were presented to the writer. And from those facts, one will choose their character, and that character will not have a choice of wisdom, wisdom derives from experience. The soul is guided by will, emotions, and mind, the mind is what make the person from that mind is the birth of the American typical Negro. But one can not escape their past, the same when one program a person, one controlled that person that's the very reason why white America controls the poor old Negro as we speak. Because they program them, the same with the wine o, the drug addict, or the teenage procreator they have been program not only to be a consumer of ignorance but to be an endowment for this here America. And one must remember that this here America was founded on a Christian religious principle all principles must surrender to reality and the typical Negro do not know what principles means. Or know the history of their great- grand parents; so, from that fact and that fact alone one can very easily see that one do not know where they come from. Now how can they know where they are going, a belief has no power here only facts survives, one can't swim where there is no water so why does one jump into a belief. We the writer will let you the reader decide for self.

Just with that scenario, if one do not know what water is how can one know they are wrong by jumping when one don't know they don't know. So by not knowing one can program one with anything all it takes is for one to believe and that's the power of belief. That why wine o drug addicts, and teenage procreators exist as we write because of the belief system. One must remember that a system entangles ones mind, and the mind is what make the person.

A belief gives one false hope, if one doesn't have the intellect to understand the meaning of a thing that one is relying on a false security. And from that false security one automatically will raise the fear of doubt then automatically becomes a wonderer a wonderer is created by the intellect of experience. If a child is a child they will act as a child, because the creation of the intellect have not arrived one could call that reason. One can very well say that is the very reason children have a problem reacting to a swimming pool because of reason. The child has been taught to believe but their intellect has out run their experience, that's the same problem the typical Negro possess as we write. Their intellect has not caught up with their information, and for that reason they suffer from a behavior disorder. That reminds the writer of that church down on Buckeye road in Phoenix Arizona that we talked about before in this book. The writer was sitting in their Sunday school the Sunday school teacher could read on a first grade or second grade level. His intellect didn't support the position he had one must remember, that a structure is no stronger than its support and must not forget that position is the greatest spot on the universe. The Sunday school class at this CO.G. I.C church we the writer is talking about the adult class could not read easy words, and the teacher would mumble over easy words. And just as soon as the writer's wife, would inform them of what the word was hey' they would take it and run with it they would even tell you what the word meant. It was as though they were asleep and was awaken by a bolt of lighting, the writer is talking about the experience in his lifetime, just think of the poor old Negro that couldn't read. White America had to teach them everything even when, how, and why. So in other words, what the writer is saying every mind has to be programmed its just don't come from above and once that person is programmed that person can be controlled by the programmer. The poor old Negro was taught by the Christian religion to obey those who have rule over you and as the writer who came from a very religious family this was very confusing. For instance, on one side of the spectrum the writer was taught to obey those who have rule over you, and on the other side of the spectrum, the same teacher that was telling you to obey was telling you it was wrong. For example, like segregated school, Negroes had to go in the back door, Negroes couldn't eat in the same room as white folks, Negroes had to set on the back of the bus, and last but not least the poor old Negro could not swear on the same bible as whites, in a court of law. Can you the reader imagine that? But, in order for the poor old Negro to get a change the Negro had to disobey, the poor old negro was program to be inferior they program their children their very own children to be inferior that is the fruits of Slavery. And as the fruits of Slavery one will automatically suffer from that effect, suffer from the effects of belonging to someone other than self. As a result of that the poor old Negro was and is a very special production that is the results of being the property of someone other than self. That trait still exists as we write, that is the very reason, that the poor old Negro is not conscience of their surrounding or do not care about the past they just want to go to sleep and forget it and hope it never returns. That why wine o's and drug addicts, exist because of the hope factor they are hoping and looking for a dream that don't exists but they keep believing. In their subconscious mind they really believe they are doing the right thing because when one is the property of another their soul belongs to another. Dr. King once said any Christian religion that is not concern about the conditions that dammed the soul is a dead dried up do nothing religion and is in need of a revolution. Now don't' get the writer wrong when he say revolution one can have a revolution of the mind, the writer is talking about a bloodless revolution. The same revolution that pave the way for the poor old Negro to be where we are as we write that's the revolution the writer is talking about. A revolution to turn the poor old Negro from the wine bottle, to turn the Negro away from drugs, to turn the teenage girls and boys from teenage procreation. A revolution that will enable the Christian religion to have a heart and a pursuit of love to have the intellect and desire that would enable them to be concerned about the conditions that dames the souls of the poor old Negro. That's the revolution the writer is talking about The writer is talking plain English, the writer is trying to spoon feed the minds of the poor old Negro. The poor old negro have been trying to adjust to the transition of adjustment every since their creation.

The picture above is the writer Tommy Charles DeHorney and the writer's mother standing behind their 1948 Chevrolet. We were showing kindness and love, Tommy mother died at his birth an at the same time Tommy's father abandon him. Where was the love? The writer's mother taught him love, and the writer tried to show love to this here Tommy. For instance, when Tommy wanted to go to college but, didn't have the funds the father would not finance the aid to college. Tommy asked the writer and the writer obliged, love is a two way affair one always have to give before they receive. So, the writer is a giving person, 'boy' he believe in planting but when Tommy's father died, Tommy didn't even take the time to call the writer. He didn't even bother to call when the writer's mother died the writer has some type of label put on his forehead or is it a curse. Or is it the writer is just not wanted for sure its' the fruits of Slavery.

Every American Negro should make it a point, to put on love my making it a point to put on love that would form a habit, from that habit, that would become a complex choice, from that choice it would become their character, from that character it would become love. From love one can grow unity, from unity, develops strength, from strength derives power, from power one can go and scope the universe. We can learn to love as a unit, or we can just die as an individual, or as Minnie would say I don't care. Whatever the decision be that decision will impact one's life, one can always ask the victim about their choice of decisions. The mind paves the way for choice; the mind derives form their genetics and the mind is still what make the person.

CHAPTER 15

JUST WHERE IS THE LOVE

IF A PERSON HAVE A African daddy and a white mother why would someone call them African American or black? Why would one scrutinize their father and disregard their mother? By not letting you know that the mother is white. Is this discrimitory, ignorance or is it just the war on women? Shouldn't the mother be recognize in this, after all the mother is the one who gave birth? Just where is the sincere for purity? The writer is talking about truth.

By not supporting the mother don't one know that society is weakling the mother one must remember that a structure is no stronger than its support, by none support one is encouraging a structure to be weak or weaken. The writer is living proof of that, which reminds the writer of his late sister Emma Jean DeHorney Sweet the mother of Rev. C.D. Sweet who is a superintendent in the church of god in Christ affiliation of Arizona In the writer's sister obituary the facts came to light that this here superintendent Sweet didn't even know his uncles name the number one son is Tommy Caldwell not Tommy Charles the writer would like to remind the readers not knowing is the most dangerous spot on the universe. The writer's father the late Rev. Julian Caldwell DeHorney said not knowing is the very reason why a wosp can't make honey a wosp can make the cone by not knowing they miss out on the honey all one has to do is think. And if one don't know asked, knowledge just don't drop from above history has plainly demonstrated that history is one's best teacher.

Now can we say that this C.D. sweet is missing something else in this family tree? Does he realize that he is the fourth generations in this here church of god in Christ affiliation?

Since the poor old Negro spirit is a wonderer by the laws of inheritance do this here C. D. Sweet wonder just what did his grandfather the late Rev Julian DeHorney contribute to this church of god in Christ affiliation? The writer wonder do C. D. Sweet realize that his grandfather use to walk 26 miles one way just to preach at a country dual purpose one room colored school every Sunday For about 2 years just to have the privilege of calling himself a country preacher, From Denison Texas to Ravenna Texas was 26 miles. C. D. Sweet grandfather didn't own a horse or car and there was no bus service and colored folks could not ride in a cab he certainly couldn't fly so, he had to do what was natural by nature walk, which was the norm for colored folks during the first 100 years of post-Slavery.

This Julian contribute three generations to the cause for this here church of god in Christ affliction. What was his pay back from the affiliation? Well the writer doesn't know the actuality of the payback but he does know the reality. When Elder Littlefield who was the pastor at the Dennison Texas Affiliation. He got killed in 1960, the church of Denison Texas wanted Julian DeHorney for their pastor. The move to get Junion Dehorney was led by the late deacon Buster Wadley but this here Bishop who last name was Hanes refused the wishes of deacon Wadley. And said he had a message from above to place his son at the church and Julian honored the bishop decision saying that the message from above was greater than that of the wishes of the members at the Denison church. Now is that obedience or what? This also shows the power of position one must remember and not forget that position is the greatest spot on the universe. So from this actual experience how can one not want to guide their children to education, education is only information it's a protector. Education has the right to protect one from Ignorance, but one must fight for their rights. By not knowing doesn't one know that their soul can be dammed and curse by the simple facts of position is not knowing inherited from the fruits of Slavery or is it just the drift of destiny? Did Junion Dehorney show love or selfishness? Did this Bishop Hanes show love or selfishness? Well with the facts on the table, the facts plainly show that Hanes showed love for his son, and showed selfness for the wants and desires for the congregation that was going to empower his son as we write that son is a Bishop in the State of Texas history has plainly demonstrated that the older Hanes was not concerned about the condition that could dammed the soul by the power he displayed no love here my friends. And this here C.D. Sweet displays the same affection for love the facts, C. D. Sweet didn't recognized the writer enough to let him know when the writer's mother died or C. D. Sweet mother and father. To top it all off the writer hadn't seen C.D. Sweet mother in 25 years so the writer took a journey to this here C.D. Sweet church to see the family and this here C.D. Sweet wife didn't even get up and come over to speak to the writer and the writer is blind. Despite the fact that her mother is 90 years plus but she got up and came over and spoke to the writer, which this was only the third time she had seem the writer from that fact and that fact alone proves the mind is what make the person. May peace be upon sister King soul. The writer will go to a parable, which was used by the late Mr. Walter Briggs who had a 2nd grade education. Who once said that the mind derives from one's principle, and the principle can only be supported by the ingredients that is available to the mind . No matter how hard one try one can't refine, reshape, or rebirth principles no matter how many times they are born again. 'Yes' Mr. Briggs also, would said he believes God take care of everything even the birds. But he have never seen God bringing worms to the birds nest, it is always the bird that go get the worm and bring it to the nest. The writer agrees the mind is what make the person. Is this love selfness or ignorance? Since every individual is born of ignorance one has to brought out of ignorance, remember Slavery that my friends is the typical Negro at its best. Which has been provided by history just where is the love. Where? The writer will tell you white America did not program his Negro children with love for self just like any person, with a behavior disorder they will have a reason for their neglect. In this case, it started with the top and ended up at the bottom as always, what ones throws up, it always comes down that's the law of gravity. Nothing lasts without a support system ignorance is no different From the actual facts that history has provided this here Christian religion that white America taught the American Negro started in 1787, has not changed only the characters and events has changed and that's the facts of reality. No paint brush here my friends, since the mind is what make the person, its what goes on inside that mind will determined, what goes on in ones life. One control another by what is put into the ingredients of the mind, the ingredients means to the mind the same thing yeast means to bread. Information broaden the mind the same thing as yeast does to the bread so therefore, one control people by keeping them ignorant just like the poor old Slave just how can one control the poor old Slave if they were not ignorant information brings a yarning to know more. Ignorance hold one back for not trying to adjust, ignorance enable one not to be conscience of their existence, with that existence people will not know there existence. How can one help that person? Does the typical Negro understand that they once were a property and now they can think for self? The poor old Negro was a treated as property, looked upon as property meaning, they had the spirit of property and the spirit is the real you. And if one do not know their existence your spirit wonders that goes to explain why the poor old Negro will be led to wine, crack and religion and any other type of abnormal behavior because they do not know where they come from their spirit is wondering the same as a sky walkers.

The poor old Negro is always wondering about their ancestors, white America did not program the Negro to keep history. They did not program them to be concern with their brother man or their mother and father, they program them to believe their pie would be in the sky their goal and their satisfactory will be in another world, not this world this world belongs to white America. So if the poor old Negro has an inquisitive mind that mind will wonder the same as the poor old Negro use to wonder in the cotton fields wondering was night ever going to come 'hey' the writer remembers just that as the writer dad use to wonder if he was ever going to get a church to support him. Or wonder why this Bishop Hanes sent his son to pastor a church over a hundred miles from where he lived. He would wonder why not me lord that's the fruits of Slavery my friends and that the typical American Negro their spirit is just a wonderer.

The fruits of Slavery support ignorance, remember a structure is no stronger than its support so by the laws of inheritance the fruits of Slavery cannot support nothing but ignorance. If ignorance is in one's mind set just where can that mind lead one in life, one cannot take another to a place and time that they are not. One can only deal with their existence for instance, if one has nothing in their hand how can they pretend they are dealing with something its only a myth my friends, and one must have the power of belief without the power of belief a myth is nothing, and a myth does not exist except in a story. A story for pre illiterate, one has to understand that this here country preacher Julion Dehorney was the first generation born out of Slavery. His mother died when he was two years old and his grandmother Hannneh raised him until he was thirteen Hanneh was a Slave for her first 25 years of life. By the way, Julion had a third grade education, at thirteen he was on his own he had to root hog or die. I am quite sure this here Hanes who Julion gave him the power to empower Julion himself did not have the same pedigree as Junion Since the intellect takes advantage of the simple. History has plainly demonstrated that Junion was obedient, that was all he knew he wanted to get on the high side of the road but didn't have the information how to obtain the high side of the road. Therefore, he existed on the low side of the road and as he procreated, he could not deliver the next generation to high side of the road. Now on the other side of the spectrum, this here Hanes had the knowledge, and desire to be on the high side of the road and looking down on the low side of the road. So just how this here Hanes derived at his position well my friends the facts would say by any means necessary. As a result of that, when Hanes procreated his creation was on the high side of the road since his son is a state bishop that's self evident.

The only thing Hanes and Junion have in common as all typical Negroes have they all derive from the fruits of Slavery it's the adjustment to the new found freedom determine the success of the typical Negro. That will determine the success of each generation, in actuality truth determine that's not a myth my friends, it seems the Christian religion is living in a generation where Christian are mastering the art of being like the world. So this here Julion Dehorney was caught in the position of not knowing and not knowing is the most dangerous spot on the universe. History has demonstrated that with Slavery for instance, the Slave was taught to be a good servant the master would by –pass Slaves and say servant to confused the mind of the Slave since the Slave didn't have no way of knowing what servant meant. White America had or has a broad definition for servant in their world it means a servant is that of a pathetic creature, virtually without will, or purpose in life, crush in spirit, bent over, liking self esteem wrinkle, weary and dirty a mindless ouch. That how the original white American describe the servant. Is that why white American taught their children different from their Negro children? The only power the poor old Negro had was to say ouch' that was the only way they could express pain or distress. Where was the love for the Africans? Where was the love for white America own children the Negro? But yet and still, white America program the Negro that Jesus is love back in the day they classified Negro as colored but they changed that. Because Negroes was not program to keep records by not keeping records one will not have pure facts of an event they will have what the poor old Negro called here say- facts.

As the generations goes on the truth will be diluted pretty soon if one do not stand up and fight for truth, the Negro will be pure African now. The poor old Negro will not have white ancestors, because one can take a paint brush and paint any picture they want. And because of the property of descent of the poor old Negro will go right alone with that plan to destroy themselves. That my friends are the very reason one decides to become a crack head, a wine o, or the descendant of deviant behavior. The poor old Negro will prepare your spirit for a place they nothing about but want even try to prepare your physical being to exist in this here white America. For instance, the Negro preacher will prepare one to receive their pie in another world but, want even try to send their own children to attend college `right here in this world. Just where is the love? Well my friends facts say that the love still exist for the property owner as the poor old Negro would say Massa' if one don't get an education the only thing one has left is that of a servant and that's a pure fact. No matter if he's' a crack head, drug dealer, or a bank teller they are all classified as a servant. Supplying the needs for the world all one has to do is think by thinking one produces a thought.

This reminds the writer of a true experience, upon graduating from high school the writer was equipped with only a willing mind and the advice from the family CEO his mother. Who advise the writer to get a job and try and make the white man the best hand he could by doing so the writer mother insured the writer that he would always have a job. But, the writer wanted more out of life than that upon discovering the love of his life Louise at the raw age of twenty Louise came to Arizona equip with a high school degree. With high hopes of meeting and marrying a man of her dreams not knowing the future she could only talk about her past. She enter the marriage with an open mind with high expectation for hope, she quickly gained the experience that hope had no value. Doing quite well after the invitation after seven years of marriage the writer had his own business two new vehicle and a house the writer applied for a loan to improve his business, to the astonishment of the lender, the lender couldn't believe what the writer owned after only seven years of marriage. Both started from ground zero with nothing, the writer remembers picking up soda water bottles, just to gain money for food. The lender asked you all own all of this at twenty seven? What in the world will you have when you get thirty five? Threw the application on the table and said point blank I can't let you have nothing and got up and left the room as if the writer had slapped him in the face that started the writer on his journey in a quest for more knowledge. As of now the writer has not been helped or encourage in his quest not to be a servant, non what –soever from outside people or his family. In fact they only put curses on the writer, the family curses still remains in tact as we write by being rejected by not only his family and the lending intuitions of Arizona the writer had no choice since he was in a position to swim of sink the writer chose the opportunity of swimming. Upon swimming the writer and his wife ended right back where she had fled, Arkansas man this was a whole new ball game the writer experience things that he hadn't even dream off. There were Negro policeman, Negro fireman, and even Negroes climbing up utility poles hey' that didn't exist in Yuma Arizona in 1971; the writer couldn't believe his eyes. This is the way of opportunity the writer had wanted all alone, even the Negroes were preaching education the writer had no education and his wife had left this place for a better future. Then, the writer met this Vietnam veteran Nathan Tidwell they became friends man all this guy talked about was education. One could tell he had been rejected by white America just by talking to this man it changed the whole life prospected for the writer. Hey' this Mr. Tidwell impacted the way the writer thought it changed the writer spirit forever in fact, if it had not been for Mr. Tidwell the writer would not be setting here writing about his experience.

Outside of Shirley and Curley Culp this Tidwell was the only person that tried to advance the writer's mental capacity the writer got a job at the same plant Mr. Tidwell was working at. Mr. Tidwell was the only Negro in the writer life experience to lobby for a position for the writer to get at the plant for the writer would be over Mr. Tidwell. Can one image that? In their wildest dreams that would be the same as a Slave who was a long time field hand lobbying for a new acquired Slave to be a cook at the big house. The writer received the promotion the writer asked Mr. Tidwell why didn't you try and get the position. Mr. Tidwell replied I am not good with numbers, all the while the writer didn't even know how to spell the name of the town we were in but the faith Mr. Tidwell displayed for the writer boosted the writer complexity to a new high that still exists as we write thanks Mr. Tidwell. Mr. Tidwell would go on to serve the company for the next thirty five years in a management position.

The experience the writer gain from that experience with Mr. Tidwell enable the writer to encourage the writer wife Louise and one of their two children to gain a college degree. The child gain two degrees, once again the writer would like to express his gratitude to his brother man Mr. Nathan Tidwell thanks for a job well done friends forever, and forever is a long time. From that experience it shows the power of unity, through unity there is strength that is the very reason the poor old Negro would say that evil doers always will try and throw a monkey wrench into the mix of unity to cause friction. Friction will always serve as a problem for instance, the writer always has a friction going on in the mix, with his family from that experience there is no unity from that unity there is no success as a family that's the fruits of Slavery. As long as ignorance, has something to feed on there will be no growth other than ignorance that's the law of nature all one has to do is think and by thinking one will produce a thought. The poor old Negro was not program to think that's the very reason why the poor old Negro and the writer's family have problem thinking because the poor old Negro was not program to think they were program to obey. The poor old Negro, does the same thing as the Christian religion does they stick with the power position who-ever- or what ever the power is that's the position both will support by that they convict themselves they are on the right side. One must remember position is the greatest spot on the universe. Do you the reader remember when the poor old Negro was set free just how this here Christian religion supported them? {not} the writer great grand mother Hanneh who was twenty five years old when they freed the Negroes said some of the Negroes didn't have shoes on their feet when they were freed only the clothes on their back no food, it was said that some of these Negroes would eat dried leaves. Now just where did the support of the Christian religion come from, their was no red cross for the poor old Negro. Do you the readers remember the victims of Katrina? Now image what it was like in 1865, after your servant was taken away from you.

The writer grew up hearing the story about freedom, that freedom wasn't free everything comes with a price tag. Can one imagine a plantation with crack head a wine o and drug dealers? That's not a possibility of an imagination one can't even imagine that a Slave would have the possibility of being a servant and a crack head. So the writer want even discuss the out of the way idea logics that would be the same as trying to imagine that someone would be on a free fall and going the wrong way. One would have to be on some good stuff, to even have an imagination like that so, the writer want even go there. But the writer will go with the Christian religion going right alone with Abe Lincoln when Abe was asked what are the poor Negroes going to do now that they are free? Abe would say it mildly The Negro would have to 'root' hog or die. The clergyman said we will pray for them the writer had a cousin whom was the first generation out of Slavery would say it plainly that prayer was alright in a prayer meeting, but it wasn't worth a dam in a bear fight. The writer heard him say just that, and his name was Jess Smith may peace be upon his soul. All typical Negroes are not religious freaks, some believe in actuality and some try to think for self. One has to remember, if the poor old Negro would obey the one who has rule over them the Negro would not be in their present position one must remember that position remains the greatest spot on the universe. The spot the Negroes possess may not be that large of a spot but it is large enough for the poor old Negro to have a selection of opportunity. They do have the opportunity to be a gick head, crack head or to think that is better than the cat of nine tails on ones ass. And by making the right choice selections the Negro now can choose there own character now if one knows it or not that's a hell of an opportunity. That opportunity did not arrive from obeying the law of the land the opportunity that now exists for the typical Negro was not available to the writer. The opportunity that existed for the writer, was prepared due to facts that existed for the writer that dammed his soul, and by his soul being dammed that automatically made his mind stagnated. The writer did not possess the will to be a college graduate nor the emotion to seek a higher education nor the mind, to think education. Now from that soul a dysfunctional being was created so the writer has to work with the soul that was prepared for him by another. Thanks to the condition that was made available to that creator that would go to explain why a person live a certain way for 18 years then, have the opportunity to go to college for 4 years and their mind set don't change. The writer is talking about the typical Negro the poor old Negro has a saying one can take the 'Nigger' out of the country but I'll be dam if one can get the country out of the 'Nigger'. That is an inherited trait from the fruits of Slavery for instance, one can take a man with a college degree and a woman with the same together they gross over a hundred thousand a year and still rent a house from white America. Then, if one try to give them wisdom they will explain why they can't accept wisdom that's' just one of many typical Negroes theory. That would be the same as with the jick head or crack head to any one whom trying to give them free wisdom that goes to explain with everything one must believe one cannot resist. Nobody in this America have graduated from any intuition and resisted every step of the way man' it just don't happen. One must receive what the professor is putting out in other words, one must believe for instance, some Negroes living in America as we write don't believe that Africans where running wild and naked in Africa at the time of the Slave trade the writer wonder what would be their explanation for gick heads and cracks lovers. The writer can only wonder since that is a non thinking mind that same person would probably say that fat meat is not greasy. People are no different from any animal we all derive from the animal kingdom one can take two of the brightest minds of any race of people except the Negro, and put them in a cage then, go out and catch two wild dogs and put them right beside them then get two well trained dogs and put them in a cage across from them and treat those animal with nothing but love nothing but pure love the two humans and the two wild dogs now the moment that they arrive everything they do wrong you beat them. If they look at you wrong beat them if they say the wrong thing beat them, if they relieve themselves on the floor and don't have no where to relieve themselves beat them. If you put there food on the floor and the humans don't eat it beat them, or if the dogs eat it beat them everything that they do wrong beat them if the humans try to think beat them if the humans don't think beat them. One doesn't have to hold them for 400 years one can hold them for six months and after six months see if their mentality change. But on the other side of the spectrum, with the trained dogs you treat them with nothing but respect and love tell them to set, rub their head when they set, tell them good dog, give them a treat When you see them in the morning rub their head, tell them what a good dog they are keep them clean water, in the summer time put ice in their water, wash their food bowl out and keep it clean. If they shake over the water tell them no bad dog, and let the other dogs and the humans see you doing that by association those humans should pick up some of that. So the tamed dogs just love them and love them, clean their teeth and tongue when a stranger comes and they bark tell them good dog and just love them. But, on the other side of the spectrum just beat them, when the human talk tell them to shut-up and beat them when the wild dog bark beat them.

When the humans relieved themselves and they don't have anywhere to relieve themselves beat them, if the human relived themselves in a corner beat them and then you asked the human why didn't you asked for a pot beat them. If they go to crying beat them if they go to pleading with you beat them. What kind of human are you going to have? Or what kind of dog will you have now will that make a human or dog love you just think for a moment, but by association they will want the same treatments that exists for the trained dogs. That would exist by association one would think. That my friends are Your American Negro they were programmed to exist in an inhumane state of mind. So, as you can see by the example, love is not automatic love has to be taught as each person will determined the material that person will serve if that person is full of ignorance that person will act accordingly if that person full of love it can only manifest love Since, love come from one's emotions and emotions derives from one soul, and the soul comes from one's will emotions and mind, and the mind is what makes the person.

The picture above, is young coach DeHorney with his first cousin the Revered C. D. Sweet. it appears C.D. Sweet is extending a hand of love to young DeHorney that lasted until the two grew into maturity. Where did the love go? That's a answer that millions of American Negroes wonder, wondering is a way of life for the poor old Negro, and they were created to wonder. It all started at fort

Jesus, and didn't end when their created father's abandon them. It was a start of a cycle that still exists as we write, C.D. Sweet received the label of the gifted one, the label that was put upon him by his grandmother Josie. Was it love? Or the knowledge of the unknown. The writer remembers C. D. Sweet growing up as a child who was about seven came over to spend the day at his grand-mother house Josie. The grand- mother asked C.D. Sweet have you eaten today? C.D. Sweet replied [Gnaw] Negro language meaning no. Then the grandmother replied do you want to eat? C.D. Sweet answer what you got. Grand mother replied I have some eggs, I don't want those old cold eggs answered C.D.Sweet grand-mother replied I have bacon and biscuits. I don't' want those old cold hard biscuits but I will take the bacon. Grand-mother replied I have some fresh light bread C.D. Sweet replied okay, that was C.D. Sweet at his best he was not taught to respect his elders. Growing -up with his mother, the writer remembers C.D. Sweet mother was against saying 'yes sir and 'yes ma'am she said she would let the child make the decision on how they would speak to older adults.

The writer could write a whole book on C.D. Sweet but will spare you the reader the details, and get to the point. C.D. sweet is just the average typical American Negro who don't know love when it hit him in the face. They love the one they should hate and hate the one they should love, history has already demonstrated that. They will hide behind the mask, which comes from their mouth that covers their true identity, this Revered C.D. Sweet didn't bother to call the writer to let him know about his father, grand-mother, or mother's death. C D. Sweet mother followed the same cycle as her mother and grand-mother Polly, as the poor old Negro would say, they all put their fruit in a bucket with a hole in it. They all died from a broken heart, history has demonstrated plainly that one can't swim where there is no water. The American Negro mind was program by the master and the mind is what make the person.

CHAPTER 16

THE POWER OF LOVE

THE POOR OLD NEGRO HAVE been beaten down mentality and physically for over 400 years the poor old Negro mind is torn up and shattered the same as if one would toss a whole egg into the air, its destroyed.

The poor old Negro don't have the existence or consciousness of their own mind, no matter where the Africans derive from whether the African was a king, queen or nomad the results are the same they are worsen by the condition they experience. History has plainly demonstrated that the condition is what dammed the soul since, the soul is what produce ones mind emotion, and will. The soul can be programmed to get a certain result just look at reality history has plainly demonstrated that with Abe Lincoln and Barrack Obama. They both was said to have Caucasian mothers and African fathers they both were raised as white unlike the writer grandfather who had an African for his mother and a Caucasian for his father. And the opportunity of being denied education but had the rights to be raised by a Slave and a ex-Slave mother since the writer's grand father mother was twenty five years old when the collar of Slavery was removed it became invisible. But the fruits of Slavery still exist as we write thanks to laws of inheritances here are few examples the writer have experience. The writer befriended his niece when she about two years old befriended is putting it mildly the writer wife treated her as if she was her own everywhere the writer's wife went she would wanted to be along side of her, people who didn't know any better thought the little girl was the writers. The little girl wanted to eat and associate every aspect of life, when the writer would take his wife and son to the Dairy queen everyday and as usual the niece was right along side. The writer never would tell her what to get he would always ask her what was she going to get the purchase price of the items did not include the nipples she was biting off her milk bottle since she was on the bottle until she was 4 years old. Not to mention the milk she was drinking that went into the bottle, never once were the writer and his wife congratulated for planting a good seed it was quite the contrary. The writer remember once how his wife complained to the baby sitter who was the writers mother about how she was biting nipple off the bottles at the expense of the writer. The writer's mother said her father can buy her some nipples and I will tell him instead of the father replacing the nipples he confronted the writer wife as if a crime had been committed. What more can one expect since this generation of people is the 2nd generation out of Slavery one has to understand the intellect had not derive to the present.

This type of behavior existed or can the writer just say it still exist as we write since none of the relatives bother to notify the writer with the passing of his brother, mother, or sister not to mention his brother - law. Is that the drift of destiny? Or can we just blame it on the fruits of Slavery, that's the typical American Negro the writer has had experience with, one has to understand when any animal is program they will react to only what they know the poor old Negro was program not to love their brother man so therefore, the typical Negro they will hate the one they should love and love the one they should hate. That type of mentality derives from fear as with any animal including the poor old Negro that animal will not bite the hand that feed them history has plainly demonstrated that with the Negro despite all of the hardship that white America have be stored upon the poor old Negro. The Negro is still white America's best friend despite the rejection and denial by white America. One can believe what they want but the facts remain the same.

White America has a saying and the poor old Negro takes it seriously the saying is there is nothing wrong with darkness the problem derive from the exposure of light They go on to say that is the reason the black man is black because they were not expose to light. Would that be the reason why the poor old Negro will not wise up? For instance, the writer's wife brother was on his death bed and the writers wife was on the phone with the sick brothers wife showing her love for her brother the brother died about two hours later the same day and the sister- law didn't have enough intellect or did any of the other family members call and tell the writer wife about her deceased brother. The writer wife heard about it by way of the grapevine two days later but when she didn't attend the Funeral it was the talk of the town, that my friends is a typical Negro. It all about perception if one is in darkness and have not been expose to light their perception will not be the same as a person who has not been expose to light That reminds the writer of a story that was handed down from Slavery the writer's great- grand mother Hannah told her master who was the father of her son. The civil war was near the end; Hannah served as a cook during the civil war for William Quantrill and his raiders while they were hiding out in wild cat thicket in Fannin County TX. William Cantrell was under the command of Hanneh master the writer great grand father. James Nolan who was a Negro and a scout for William Cantrell told Hannah that he was a free Nigger, and told Hanneh what it meant to be free. With Hanneh new found information she confronted her master with the news about soon to be freedom. Her master told her you haven't got the slightest clue what freedom means. In other words, what the writer's great grand father was saying that Hanneh didn't have the correct perception of freedom? The poor old Negro would say that perception boils down to choice by doing nothing most people do not understand that doing nothing is a choice. Just as is this Merarion who is the writer's wife sister-law made her choice of not calling in other words, she done nothing about the situation. As the writer's great grand father E.L. would say she Merarion has a perception of nothing just what is nothing? Can one imagine what nothing is? Can one develop nothing? Jesus said it best a tree is known by the fruit it bears. For example, when one is in darkness one has to have the image of light, in order to be developed the same as an athlete the poor old Negro is no different one has to be exposed to light before one can be developed into light. The image is there by the laws of inheritance, a good example would be a cross between the African and white American that individual which was produce from the image of the African and white America lies dormant until developed. That is the law of nature now from that image if white America breeds back into that image and that image is developed would that image be a yellow skin Nigger like the writer. From the facts, that is produce by history how can that picture be black the fact of the matter would produce the law of nature and that nature would produce the majority which will be a light skin Nigger. But on the other side of the spectrum there's ignorance, and ignorance has to be fed to maintain its quality So by being injected with fear, fear bring doubt , from doubt create the perception of nothing and nothing is very satisfying to the mind set for white America for the poor old Negro that's the very reason that a yellow skinned Negro have the perception that they are black in actuality they have a perception of nothing. That's why a Negro will develop themselves into a gick head, a crack head, or just a preacher the majority of them will lead you to nothing all one has to do is look at their resume it will set the record straight. The same as the truth will set you free or a tree is known for the fruit it bear. But, their are some exception to the rule the writer will explain the exceptions are so few and in between it's as though they don't exist. For instance, the writer drove a commercial truck for 26 years.

Where did the light come from to develop that fact? Did the writer go to school to gain the knowledge to drive the truck? Was it magic? Was it a miracle? Guess what it was a jick head; just what is a jick head? A jick head is a word derive from the poor old Negro it slang for a drunk. Normally a jick head is a person that works all week and gets drunk on the weekends who want to take off on Monday's. A jick head don't have a perception of which his family is also, a jick head will take his pay check and gamble his pay check off. A gick head don't have any respect for his children in other word, a gickhead is just a simple nothing. The writer's great grand father would say a jick head is just matter taking up space. But that gick head is the one who taught the writer how to drive a commercial truck. In essence what the writer is saying the gick head showed more compassion for love than the so- called bible toting Christian who stood by and did nothing for the writer. As the results of the gick head the writer's family was blessed by the blessing of the gick head.

This is a parable that derives from Slavery; the poor old Negro is caught between the heads of a two –headed snake the snake being lodged between the north and the south. The snake has bit the nigger in the ass and is holding on to that bite like a pit bull the poor old Negro is on their hands and knees, eyes bucked and mouth open just waiting on their command. That's where the Negro DNA derives from since DNA is the cause for every reaction if one would follow their root system it the root system will go all the way back to their genetic pool. The poor old Negro is no different the poor old Negro do not have one set of mentalities, since mentalities is the total sum of a persons intellectual capabilities the poor old Negro have multi mentalities Why? Because they derived from all types of genetics for instance, some Slaves were housed in an arena type house. Some Slaves had their own cabins some Slaves shared building; some Slaves had building for the men and houses for the women. Now this was the type of plantation the writer's great-grand- mother Hannah came from some Slaves lived in a family type setting some plantation segregated the blacks from the yellow some plantations let the blacks live together as a community but had a house for the yellow women. And they called it the yellow house it was out of bounds for the black men and it would be close to the big house. And it was preserve for yellow women only. Often they would take the children from the yellow house and they would be raised in the big house. Now you the reader, know who the father of the children where the yellow skin of their body tells one that, so one can see that with all these different types of mind sets one will have many types of mentalities.

That is where and how the typical Negro derives from. The poor old Negro is a multi- type individual for instance, the writer remembers the old Smith plantation down in Fannin county TX. The Smith's where very rich and it was another family down in this neck of the woods by the name of Boatwright who was very poor. The Boatwright's didn't have any servants because of their economic status in the summertime; the kids didn't wear shoes, shirts, or underwear. One could pass by their house pigs would be on their front porch or under the house goats could be seen standing in the window. They would remove their windows during the summer months for air circulation. Now do you the reader, think if a Negro came from the Boatwright plantation would have the same mentality as one comes from the Smith's plantation. It was said and is documented that when the Negro was freed the Smith's plantation gave its Nigger children 75 acres of land but on the other side of the fence the Boatwright type plantation kept the shoes the Negroes were wearing. Now can you the reader distinguished between the two mentalities. Would that be a cause for a difference in genetics? Of course it would that's the typical American Negro that is the very reason why the poor old Negro have two heads one for the Negro and one for white America. Some Negroes would prefer one to say they have two different types of coats one for cool weather and one for cold weather. When and what –so- ever the case may be the results come out the same, meaning the poor old Negro would have two different personalities. All for the same reason the reason being genetics and that genetics will explain the three types of characters the writer will talk about the characters being Nathan Tidwell, John Harmon, and Henry Shanklon. Mr. Tidwell who played a vital part in establishing the writer as we know him as we write. Mr. Harmon gave a helping hand alone the way and Mr. Shanklon showed the Boatwright effect. The writer has already explain the effect that Mr. Tidwell had on the writer progress for humanity but haven't explain how Mr. Harmon contribution contributed to the writer' journey. Mr. Harmon told the writer if the Negro didn't possess two heads they would be like a one handed person in other words, they would be handicapped. That reminds the writer of a story, that was handed down from Slavery their once was a master who own a Slave the master won the Slave in a card game. The master was a liberal he believe in living and let live but he won the Negro in a card game and he became his property. The master was a gambler and it was in his blood the master daddy was a gambler so by nature and inheritance the master was a natural born gambler. The town people thought the gambler had money in actuality, he just knowed how to make money so when he obtained the Slave he had to figure out how to make the Slave fruitful. Back in the day everything was plentiful including the poor old Negro, everyone trusted everyone except the poor old Negro but the poor old Negro was a Slave the poor old Negro would grow the food, harvest the food, and cook the food for master. If need be, the Slave would feed the master that's how loyal and loving the typical Negro is. But when it comes to trusting the first thing white America would say you can't trust a Nigger and at the same time, white America is laying up sleep and that good Nigger is watching over them. Often times without even a lock on their door. Getting back to the story of the gambler the gambler figure out a job for his new found Slave the Slave grew a garden kept the house cooked, and raised animals for their fresh meat.

Just what would the job be, the job would be to steal yes' steal remember white America taught the Negroes everything they know including stealing. 'Say what' yes didn't white America steal America from the red man? One can just say white America wrote the book on psychological warfare, deceptions and greed. So stealing would be and is an easy task, back in the day most merchants would receive their goods early in the morning before the merchants open. So what the gambler would do he would take his horse drawn wagon and have his Slave load the wagon with goods from the merchants. Most merchants didn't miss any goods because of the trust factors; because the majority of the merchants were uneducated they had a problem counting anything over ten. And the merchants would receive their goods on consignment that is a practice that still exists as we write. Could that be the reason there is no Negro merchants as we write because people were taught not to trust the Negro? One must remember discrimination has to be programmed it is not an inherited trait; history has plainly demonstrated that with the Negro mammy. It was said it would be as many as four babies nursing on the poor old Negro mammy at the same time during Slavery. The Negro mammy would nurse master baby alone with other Slaves babies to free the Negro women for they could work. One has to remember, that Slavery was a business not an opportunity for the poor old Negro, now let's get back to the gambler. Back in the day education was not the norm, as it is as we write form the warehouse to the delivery man and by time the merchants got it one can assure there would be no correctness in the numbers. That is the reasons the where house would provide extras for shrinkage they called it in essence, it was the pure case of not being politically correct. So the gambler would have his Slave to get a little bit of this and a little bit of that one could very well say that the gambler was taking advantage of the so called shrinkage. The writer remember himself when one could buy a 24 pack of soda pops the merchant would throw in a extra bottle for good measures quite the contrary as we write. Getting back to the gambler the gambler was not only a gambler but a horse trader the gambler was a liberal, he also, kept a fancy woman by his side. The gambler treated his Slave more like a human than a Slave; he taught the Slave how to play cards and even drank whiskey with the Slave. He even accused the Slave of impregnated his white woman since the Slave was about as white as he was it was some questions about the child. The Slave didn't like to steal he would often tell his master about stealing one day the gambler had his Slave steal some fur peps from a trapper after that un explains things started to happen to the gambler. For instance, a store house was burn down, fences were cut, and some of his life stock was missing things that puzzle the gambler. So one day the Slave told the gambler he knew what was happening to the things the Slave would go on to say they stole from the wrong person. Because the Slave knew the trapper and all the gambler had to do was to give the fur back to the trapper and the problem would be solved. So the gambler told the Slave to go and talk to the trapper and the Slave obeyed. The trapper told the Slave to bring the goods back and the Slave obeyed. When the Slave brought the goods back the trapper would not let the Slave leave in other words, the trapper stole the Slave. The gambler didn't have the gall to get the Slave back so the Slave became the trapper Slave. The trapper was not only a trapper but a horse trader, so the Slave did everything he cooked, clean house, grew a garden, and raised animals for food and trained the trapper's horses. The trapper was a bible toting Christian and a believer his belief was so strong that he favored a belief over reality. The Slave didn't like the trapper because the Slave had to stay in the storage house plus the trapper wouldn't, let the Slave drink whiskey. The Slave was afraid of the trapper but was more afraid of running away the trapper didn't understand how good a horse trainer the Slave was. The most important thing the trapper didn't understand was that the Slave was what the poor old Negro would called a two –headed nigger. The Slave had one head for his master and one head for self, and self was an individual and self thought like an individual. Meaning when one is an individual they Disguise them as an individual to say the least the trapper was not an educated thinker he was not a tomorrow's people. Tomorrows people are advance thinkers and the Slave being a distinguish person that meant he was separated from the trapper. By obeying the trapper that confused the trapper that made the trapper think that he was like any other Slave. And by the trapper thinking that way that made the trapper thoughts, only a possibility at best the majority of the people think like that. The writer has a brother who thinks like that but as we will learn its two sides to every coin, and each mind set has a mind of its own. The mind is what separate people as we will find out about this Slave because the trapper had faith in his Slave and believed in him. Because he let the Slave cook for him and trained his horse's, he believe in his Slave the trapper believe it was only one mind at work. So, one morning as the trapper was on his way to church the trapper went and told the Slave to saddle his favorite horse and the Slave obeyed. The trapper got on the horse and rode off about a hundred yards from the house the Slave yell out to the horse and the horse began to pitch and threw the trapper off. Once the trapper fell to the ground the horse began to trample the trapper, the horse trample the trapper until his death. The moral of the story is ones, life is in the hands of the beholder in other words, it's what they believe and once they make their choice its like pouring milk out of a jug. Once the choice is made history has demonstrated one cannot pick-up spill milk the Trapper could identity with that if only he was alive, or would the trapper say the slave kissed him before the slave kicked him.

Mr. Harmon stated that the poor old Negro could not be successful and be honest with their owners. Therefore, the poor old Negro had to find a solution for progress. For instance, it was said during the civil war some of the plantation owners would just kill the Negroes if they seemed jubilated about the civil war. Some owners would just walk up to the poor old Negro and blow their brains out that's right, that alone would dis- encourage anyone from thinking out loud. By that fact and that fact alone the Negro would understandably have to develop a system for self and one for their master. If the poor old Negro want to progress, the key word is want so therefore, the poor old Negro would have to develop a system for thinking for self. Mr. Harmon would go on to say, when a Negro go to the bank for a loan when the loan officer called you for an interview always wear a hat. When called in for the interview take your hat off and balled it -up as though it was nothing, always wear shoes no boots and no socks, pulled up your pants legs after you have been seated, so the officer can see you are not wearing socks. Be very polite and laugh at everything they say just as if you were nothing because that's the way they want you to be. Mr. Harmon in actuality does not wear socks. Why? Because it was handed down to him that the plantation his people derived from were not allowed to wear socks. So he dedicated his life to that cause in remembrance of his ancestors as we write Mr. Harmon is the owner of a mortuary in Tyler Texas. The writer remembers in 1979, the writer was laid off- from work and he went to a freight company to apply for employment and the lady told the writer they were not hiring. So, the writer was disappointed and disoriented and was ready to give it up, he the writer decided to call Mr. Harmon and told him the problem. Mr. Harmon replied De. You go right back up too that freight company and go in the back door just like you own the company. Go to the second door on the right and asked for Mr. Fugate and tell him that old John Harmon sent you. The writer done just that Mr. Fugate replied what can I do for you? The writer replied I need a job old John Harmon sent me. Mr. Fugate replied where do you want to go to work Amarillo or El Paso, the writer replied Amarillo. Can you be there in the morning said Mr. Fugate? The writer replied yes' sir and Mr. Fugate gave the writer an application. Then the writer was told to fill it while he found a truck for the writer to take a road test in. That's the power of love the same power of love the Smith's had for their Negro children. Thanks Mr. Harmon may you continue to have success at your mortuary, hold off on the writer if you can.

On the other side of the spectrum, this here Henry Shanklon had always called the writer telling the writer if ever he needed any help just let him know. One time the writer decided to take him up on his offer, the writer went to school with him and worked with Mr. Shanklon and had even given him a helping hand, a hand of love. So the writer asked Shanklon to get Frank Culp telephone number since Shanklon said he went right by Franks house to this day as we write Shanklon have not called or been heard from since. The writer said all of that to say this it's the mentality of the plantation owner that served as a teacher for the poor old Negro.

Mr. Tidwell and Mr. Harmon derived from a plantation of honesty, care, and joy. It can be that Shanklon derived from the Boatwright effect need the writer say any more.

The picture above is the writer's family missing his only sister the lady is Josie, behind her is her precious son Thurman. And the one carries the label the main ingredient next to Thurman is Tommy Caldwell the writer is the one with the fro', in front of the writer is a white man. We all call him dad even Josie missing is Emma Jean. At the time of the picture Josie was seventy -four Emma Jean was present for the picture but refuse to take the picture. This was the only opportunity for Josie and Julion would ever have to be present with their adult children, or quite possibly ever and ever is a long time.

One could say, this was a history making moment but by her refusing to take the picture it was shattered. We can only wonder why Emma Jean refused, any excuse is unacceptable. Excuses go back to the root of ones principles, no love equals any unity, and where there is no unity one will always find no power. Power is powered by the mind, and the mind is what make the person but the mind is powered by the spirit, and the spirit is the real you. One don't understand the power of the spirit, the spirit decides one's choice, choice like being a crack head or a preacher. The choice derives from the soul, if the soul is dammed the spirit is automatically shattered. The poor old Negroes soul, were dammed by the conditions that was available to them. Their spirit were shattered by the inheritance of the soul, one cannot fix nothing that is shattered they can only reconstruct a shattered thing one can fix something that is broke, but not something that is shattered. Try to fix shattered glass; one can only wonder what if. The first act to any stimuli should be peace and love not an argument but the typical American Negro love to argue. That's the results of the evil spirit, the purpose is to still your joy, and a joyful spirit creates a joyful thinking. Consistent love make no sense to a person with a developmental problem, one can't live by their feelings, feelings change we live in a changing society. One's feelings will eventually catch- up with your decisions fear is the power of darkness.

Ones attitude and principle will always direct one's future, the Negro hold anger toward their creation, that's the very reason they display anger toward another Negro they want them to fill what they feel. That's the results of a curse that was dispatched upon the poor old Negro that's the results of a shattered spirit that developed from the fruits of Slavery. Negroes do not fear another Negro but they do fear their master they want to show how obedient, kind, and loving they are because of the power of fear.

One can easily tell their enemy, because the enemy will try and steal your joy.

CHAPTER 17

A TREE IS KNOWN FOR THE FRUIT IT BEARS

THERE WASN'T A FINER PARABLE than when Jesus said a tree is known for the fruit it bears.

With that in mind two scenario comes to surface, for instance, you the reader have two people working in the office one of the office worker's mother was an office worker

And born and raised in an office, the other person just did Nigger work picking cotton, chopping cotton, picking peaches, and cleaning up etc.... Which do you the reader believe would make the best office worker? The one that was born in an office or the one that grew up during odd jobs 'yes you the readers are ever so- right. By association alone paves the way for a mole to be established, and from that mole a perception is born. One must remember and must not forget, one must start and develop a habit, from that habit, and a character is developed. One must remember that the mind is what makes the person, one's power lie in their mind set; but the will of the person has authority to rule.

Without the will in actuality the mind is useless, as the writer's great - grand- father would say its just matter just taking up space. That reminds the writer of another scenario, the writer knew this guy from Hope Arkansas he was an acquaintance of the writer and Mr. Tidwell never did know his name because he refuse to give his name so the writer just called him Dick. One day the writer and Mr. Tidwell were going to Hope and told Dick that the writer and Mr. Tidwell would like to visit his home. This Dick stood up and said that 'he didn't want us coming by his house." The writer asked why not? Dick replied man I might not be home and when I leave home I tell my wife not to answer the door. And the writer asked why? Dick replied man my wife wear lots of short dresses around the house and when she walks she moves a lot of body parts. Man I don't trust no man alone with my wife. Man you just don't tease a hungry dog with a steak then, Dick went on to say trust has broken -up a many home. And I myself don't plan on trusting a man alone with my wife, man I love that woman and I want to keep it just as it is.

Man I would trust you with my life, but not with my wife.

Now this here Dick was just straight and plain, hey that's the only way to be so say's Mr. Walter Briggs the truth, will set you free and enjoy your retirement Dick.

From that experience, with Dick one can tell that his soul was built on a solid foundation he ranks rights up there with the best of the writer's acquaintance, people like Jesse Nunn and Monroe Morrison. Man this Monroe Morrison was a man among men the late Monroe Morrison he was a character and would do anything he could to help a brother man. He would go out of his way to give you a hand of love, he chewed Tobacco, and dipped snuff at the same time, and said if you give me a drink of whiskey I will drink it now. He was a tough character the writer would not be in the position he is in today if it was not for Monroe Morrison. He took education to a new level saying one person could not know too much, and a penny saved is a penny earned. He also said by not knowing was like sitting on a time bomb, sooner or later that time bomb will go off. So, by not knowing that could cost you or your love one your life, so learn all you can. The more one learn the more wisdom one will have to rely on. He would also say open your mind to understanding, not devilment Mr. Morrison is greatly missed by the writer and may peace be upon his soul.

You know life is like a journey especially, for the typical Negro, it has been a long hard and rough journey. Especially to get to the point where the Negro are as we write life is no different than getting on the highway say on the west coast, and driving all the way to the east coast. The writer can guarantee that you will run into some bad roads and for sure some highway construction. It's impossible to drive coast to coast without any down time due to mal-function; life is the same way for the plain old Negro. The poor old Negro haven't gotten any help for their success, the writer knows very well that some people would say otherwise. But, the writer does have history on his side; the Negro has had pure hell gaining his position in life. Man you have white folks against the Negro, Negro against the Negro, children against their parents, self against self; but the only help the poor old Negro have received came from above. For instance, the writer was living in Arkansas which was the worst time of his life wearing shoes that was wore out by his son and passed on down to the writer. He could not work because of an accident the writer's wife was working on her degree from the University of Arkansas, the car had broken down and we had no money.

The writer called upon the church although, the writer didn't ask the church for help, the church could only pray for him. Out of the clear blue sky, this Jesse Nunn called one Sunday morning although; the writer didn't consider Mr. Nunn a friend or even a good acquaintance. Mr. Nunn came through not only as a absolute friend but that of a pure soul brother. Not even the writer's blood brother would do or have did what Mr. Nunn did when he called he asked how the writer was doing. The writer told Mr. Nunn his problems although the writer doesn't like to share his problems with other people nor, is the writer a beggar. The writer has a lot of pride the writer would not dare ask his siblings for help it would be a waste of time so why bother. Even though, the writer had helped them.

But after telling Mr. Nunn about his problems he asked how is your wife getting to school while you don't have a car in working order? The writer replied anyway she can short of begging, Mr. Nunn is a certified mechanic who worked the night shift and he said we must get this car running for your wife can finish school. The writer told Mr. Nunn he had no money for repairs, since the repair would require going inside the motor. Mr. Nunn replied money is not the issue here; the issue is the car need to be repaired so your wife can finish college. Mr. Nunn was true to his word he didn't profess to be any type of believer as he would describe it. He was a just skirt chasing, whiskey drinking man that drove a Cadillac. He learned his trade on a plantation; a old white fellow taught him the trade. Mr. Nunn said the old white fellow told him I am going to give you something that will last you for life. And don't ever say that white folks have never done anything for you because if you do you will be lying. This Jesse Nunn told the writer the same thing but instead of saying white folks Jesse said nigger. So, the writer can only say thanks Jesse Nunn for a job well done that's one of many typical Negroes who didn't forget where they came from. Unlike, some typical Negroes who want to forget their past, which comes from the hood and gain fame both on the athletic field and the movie sets who run through airports in their spare time and was the envy of many American only wishing their children to be like the superstar. Many Negroes name their children after him only to take his fame and fortune and give it to opposing side. He got caught up in the wrong position then ran back to the hood looking for help from the poor old Niggers the ones he turned his back on. And the poor old Negro came through for him again and got him out of trouble and put him back on easy street and would say he deserve a second chance. But, the poor old Negro just don't learn from experience, now instead of asking one what's your name he's asking what's your number. As the poor old Negro would say some Negroes just don't believe fat meat is greasy, history has plainly demonstrated that it is. Now on the other side of the spectrum, here is this beloved brother Ron Jesse who was part of the good time gang in Yuma Arizona the good time gang were the writer, Willie Meeks, Mike Bundy, and Ron Jesse. The writer was a senior of the bunch, who would hang out in the hood together go to Ponce's grocery store jacking food.

We would Jack food from Ponce's market, and go to Willie's house to cook the food, this Mike Bundy thought he could really cook eggs his best was just mediocre to the writer Although the writer is not bragging it just good old country facts, of course Mike would disagree with that.

Willie became a mortar for the country he died before his twenty -second birthday in a foreign land for a cause he knew not why. After Willie's death the writer found out that Willie was his best friend, at the time of his existence the writer did not have the intellect to know that Willie was a dear friend, may peace be upon his soul. Mike Bundy died before his fiftieth birthday he was sequestered to the worlds greatest known disease may peace be upon his soul. We all played on the same basketball team in high school Willie Meeks was the long shot artist, and Mike Bundy was the fancy passer. He would often hit the writer in the head because the writer wouldn't see the ball coming. The writer didn't educate his instincts to know that Mike was a super passer. The writer was the rebound expert and the enforcer, some people would call him a bully, but the writer just wanted to make his presents known. Now on the other side of the spectrum, this Ron Jesse he wanted it all whatever, it was he wanted it. Whether it was on the court or off the court he just wanted to be the best. Since the mind is what makes the person one can very well say, That Ron Jesse let his mind educate his spirit to be the best at whatever he was doing. For instance, Ron Jesse played in the NFL for 11Years and the writer will always remember Ron Jesse for the hit he took from Jack Tatum coming across the middle. Tatum knocked him unconscious after he caught the ball his concentration was so intense, they had to pry the ball out of his hands while laying unconscious on the ground. So from that fact and that fact alone one can say that this here Ron Jesse mind educated his hands to hold on to the ball and that derives from wanting to be the best. And that desire made him one of the best wide receiver's to ever play the game not bad for the guy that wasn't wanted out of high school.

That reminds the writer, of a time we were playing a basketball game against an all white team, the first half was coming to an end. The writer made his present known while grabbing a rebound as the buzzer sounded. The writer were surrounded by four white boys, and they started to knock the writer around the writer had not went to his offence, in fact the writer was looking for a place to escape. All of his teammates had disappeared except, Ron Jesse and he came to the rescue as a brother that was in need that was the type of courage Ron Jesse had. Eleven years in the NFL did not change him one bit that's the perception the writer received Jesse was straight and plain. The late Mr. Walter Briggs said when a man is straight and plain he can't give anymore'. Ron proves his loyalty more than the writer tends to discuss. So, the writer will spare you the reader of the details Ron died before he became sixty and may peace be upon his soul.

To reach a conclusion, on the typical Negro the poor old Negroes comes in many shapes and forms, some big, some little, some fat, some skinny, some very black, with nappy hair, some very black with curly hair, some black with straight hair, some brown with curly hair, some brown with nappy hair you name it the Negro has it. If you imagine it can be found in the Negro race my friends, it seems that is what make the Negro so distinct it all boils down to one thing the poor old Negro just don't have a country.

Because it is black folks all over the world but they call them something other than black. Just as the poor old Negro would say, just as many shapes and forms the Negro derive from each one is an individual. And each one has it own mind, some creative and some the minds are very dysfunctional, to put it mildly. 'Man you can take one snake and two Nigger they both would see the snake differently, one would see it as evil, and the other may see it as a blessing. But for sure one can almost be certain when two Negroes starts talking about the snake it will be for sure they sound like they are talking about two different snakes.

That's the very reason; the writer used so many illustrations describing the typical Negro because each poor old Negro has their own mind set. That the very reason the Negroes does not come as a unit they were created to be separate and 'hey man that's putting it mildly.

It seems, as if the poor old Negro cannot exist as a unit and it seems as they will never change in a life time they just cannot make the transition Why? Was it because they were created to be that way? Or was it because the Negro was programmed with brutality and white America turned their back on humanity? Or was it just the drift of destiny. There wasn't a finer parable when Mr. Wiley Golden said that the poor old Negro is just like a wild deer from Beirne Arkansas. They will always follow the one in the lead so from that whatever goes on in their Negro mind set will determined what will go on in their life. Because the poor old Negro was created to be a follower, the poor old Negro will not try and see things as they are the Negro has a problem thinking for self history has already demonstrated that. If one would just pull up the poor old Negroes resume even if it is light for the Negro can see for self they will feel more comfortable asking someone else to make the decision. They really have faith in a belief, man they love the Santa- Claus affect, and they love magic, but can't tell you how magic works they love to trust the unknown. And 'hey man trust has broken -up a many home and white America, loves that part of the position the poor old Negro is in as we write. One can control anything with trust if you have that trust you can control that thing and trust derives from ignorance and by being ignorant you can control a people that's how it is done here in America.

This is done in the religious sector the poor old Negro would read a sentence from the bible and will interpret it one way. Then, white America will come along and interpret it another way. And the poor old Negro will never argue with white America, but, will argue over the same thing with another Negro.

The writer's father always compared the poor old Negro with the wild horse and would say that a wild horse was useless, until one could put a harness on it. You know something he was ever - so right and he only had a third grade education. Can you the reader in your wildest dreams imagine catching a wild African running wild and naked, then take them home and put them in kitchen and tell them what you want for dinner. What results do you think one would get? Yes the same you would get if you catch a wild horse and throw a harness on the horse, whatever that come natural that would be the results. The same with any child, when a child starts to walk one has to break the spirit of any animal before that animal would obey. Why do you think the penitentiary is full? Why do you think some people still eats people in the twenty - first century? It all about the spirit since the spirit is the real you. Ones' spirit lies lodged between the positive and the negative meaning, it has the choice to go either way. That reminds me the writer of his grandmother who once said that the poor old Negro had two spirits one evil one good. She was born Polly Jones her mother and father were ex- Slaves Polly mother died from child birth. Polly's father rejected her upon her arrival at that time in America there was no child protected service. Her brother whom we wrote about in this book was named Ruben Phillip's that was her half brother. She was born in around 1880, Ruben tried to raise her for the first ten years or so but she became to head strong for him. So at about the ripe old age of ten she became a woman she did whatever it took to survive and the writer never did see her smile or laugh. She use to set on the porch and tell stories about the past, while she was telling stories about the spirits, the good spirit and the evil spirit. Then, she would go on to say that a good spirit was a smart spirit and an evil spirit was an ignorant spirit Since, evil is the same as ignorance it does one no good ignorance is evil. But Polly would go on to say ignorance is available to the one that wants it.

The writer late sister Emma Jean asked Polly one day which spirit do you possess grandmother? Polly looked Emma Jean right in the eye without cracking a smile she said boldly and proudly I am the one that I feed. In essence, that is the way it is with all animals the same can be said about the elephant, the elephant is real strong in the wild but once you break their spirit one can control them with a very small stick. History has plainly demonstrated that with the poor old Negro, they are no different remember the African came to America in chains. White America breed them down to a Negro and now they can control them with their tongue and a pencil, man that is downsizing. Would that go to say what one feed one determines their mental growth? Or could one just say, that the poor old Negro cannot master their circumstances, because they were created to let the circumstances master them, the poor old Negro.

The constitution of this here U. S. was written in 1776; in this here constitution it describes the poor old Negro as three fifths of a people. Not once have the writer, heard about a disagreement from that description from the poor old Negro community. So, one can assume that is accepted by the Negro community even though, assumption is only a possibility at best but the writer is only writing about what we have facts to back up our writing. Can it be safe to say, that the Negro community really looks upon these groups of men as their founding fathers or creative father since the American Negro was created right here in this America. They were created for America, and by the so- called American to be used as property, one must not forget that.

And should one believe and obey their creative fathers, and in 1776, the poor old Negro had not reached the status and responsibility to serve a God other than their creative fathers so says history and history don't lie. One can safely say that history is not a casualty of a belief one must remember and cannot forget that the poor old Negro was not taught Christianity until 1787. Was it because of the three fifths of a human? Was it because one is three fifths of a human does that mean they cannot be reason with?

Can one say that the reason the Negro community don't say anything about this here three fifths is because they are happy to be three fifths. Or is it they don't know what three fifths really means? And where did this three fifths derive from, and what formula was use to reach this conclusion? Knowing white America as history has describe they have facts too back up their theory. Did it come from the Bible? Was the original man who is believed to be the black man creative right alone side the so- called white man? If you the reader, believes yes' so in essence, what you are saying is a dog can derive from a Jackal, or a cat from a lion that's impossible my friends under the laws of hereditary descent. The same as one can't derive a white person from an African type 'please don't appeal to a miracle to escape this dilemma. Because that is the typical way The poor old Negro will do it, and will say it was god sent, halleluiah and glory to god.

The picture above is that of the Revered Doyle Moore and wife the late Brenda Moore holding son David. Doyle is holding Doyle Jr. and this picture is to illustrate the classification of color. As one can plainly see Doyle and Brenda cannot be classified as the same color or the same. Knowing is stronger than hearing that's the purpose of this picture, to know the difference between black and light skin.

There's no such thing as a light skin black that's a myth, the same as Santa Claus. No light skin person should describe themselves as black in essence, that's not only ignorant that's unjustified to self, falsehood derives from misconception. Misconceptions identifies the wrong view meaning the idea is a view of what someone other than self want, in other words, they are misleading you to misguide if one is in the dark they will follow.

Light conquers darkness, light skin do not derive from dark skin, Negroes derive from their creative father White America all on has to do is think. The mind is what makes the person not obedience's.

The above picture is it white or black? Its neither it's just the typical so-called American Negro. The picture is that of the late Emma Jean De Horney -- Sweet the writer's late sister. She was the pride and princess of her mother Josie. She was not only beautiful, she was a pianist, a seamstress, and she tailored all of her clothes. All of this which started at around the young age of ten, a trade that was handed down from her mother Josie.

She made the co-author wedding dress, and she was one of a kind and we miss her deeply with all honesty. She was just a misfortune by being a victim of the fruits Slavery. The writer can only describe her as being very complex, may peace be upon her soul

The author:

CHAPTER 18

THE FINAL CHAPTER E.L.

SINCE THIS IS THE BOOK'S last chapter we will try to make it the best.

As one should know one's principle will always surrender to reality, the writer bases his facts on truth. Since truth will set one free, if one use truth as a base there is no reason to hide. As Mr. Walter Briggs would say, by using truth as a guide one will always be straight and plain. It's a known fact; a coward is a liar, just as the Sun provides energy to the Universe truth provides absolute for the pure. No one that is alive on this Universe knows for certain on how or when the Universe derived, they just take it as they find it, and proclaim how it all started. But it's only a possibility at best, and it's not a clear possibility only someone other than self original thought. Heaven only knows where that thought derive from one can only wonder, but we do know by the laws of history that the human kind have serve an apprenticeship of prehistoric existence. Or can we just say a primitive state of mind. Where did that primitive state of mind derive from? My friends it derives from not knowing'. Now the question would be who is responsible for mankind's development? Can we appeal too miracles? Or can we just say it was the drift of destiny

And destiny is a predetermined unknown another question have arrive a question by absolute the American Negro can't answer. Why? Because the poor old American Negroes ancestors went over two hundred years without the aid of a religion. What were they believing in? So, from that fact and that fact alone the poor old American Negro cannot be an expert on religion due to the experience factor, one must realize that the poor old American Negro did not receive schooling for religion until 1787, religion was out of bound for them so by that all American Negroes are in limbo to absolute they can only be thankful for the drift of destiny. Pure facts derive from history, without actuality history serves only as a belief, and a belief is only as strong as it support. And since religion is not an inherited trait one must wonder, and wonder is only a possibility at best.

A principle serves an idea to an individual, and all principles must surrender to reality then, it becomes a fact.

The writer grew up in the church as we stated before, the writer's father was a country preacher and why do we say country because when one is country ones has country principles just by association, And just with association one must surrender to reality one cannot exist in ignorance and have the principles of a Harvard graduate that's against the laws of nature. The mind is what make the person, genetics and association is the ingredients for the mind. From that fact and that fact alone we the writer can move on to the base of this scenario, in the beginning of time how many creations were there according to the holy bible. From the facts of actuality, no one knows for certain all one can do is wonder the same as the American Negro they wonder about their ancestor, its American Negroes living as we write know they have a grandmother but don't know the grandmothers name or grandfathers name. The grandmothers and grandfathers have helped these Negroes have provided food and shelter for them but couldn't produce their names if there life depended on it we the writer is talking about educated Negroes with college degrees they are just not concerned with their past. But will try to sale you a bill of goods to another world, hey' that sound like some Negro preacher.

The mind is what make the person, that's a known fact and that mind derives from their genetics and surrounding. One can take a Negro it does not matter if there from the ghetto, hood, or country and train those to be an entertainer, to perform but their innateness will remain that's because of their originality. Meaning their genetics will be intact, or they will lie dormant until they surrender to reality. For instance, one can hear about a super entertainer who will do the simplest of things such as, following someone ignorant, or driving drunk. After they have showcase their position, they will surrender to their innateness which is ignorance. The poor old American Negro had a saying one can educate a Negro but they will never get the ignorance out of that Negro. Can that explain why an educated Negro doesn't know their grandparents names? Or was it because the original Negro was programmed to serve, perform, and be an endowment for this here America.

So, if one given an opportunity on a silver platter one should accept just as the writer' great grand father left an opportunity for all open minded people too think for self.

Here is the way the former slave owners had their perception of the beginning of time.

We the writer will go the king James version and in Genesis we find that god first made the grass to grow, then the herbs and afterward the fruit trees. Then preceding to animal kingdom, made first the fishes, then the fowls of the air and afterward the beast of the field. And closing his glorious work with the creation of man.

If the position already taken as to the creation of types and species be correct, it follows that each distinct type of man was the subject of a separate creation. Either directly or indirectly through operations of the laws of nature, which laws are probably beyond finite comprehension. In the progressive order of God's plan creation, the lowest type of man would naturally follow. Next after the gorilla or the ourang-outang. Beginning with the lowest form of human life the creative plan proceeded in progressive order from lower to higher types through the Australian, the Papuan, the African and the Mongolian until the highest type Adam. He was created Governor of the earth, and the federal head and representative of all the types and families of men. And was placed in an earthly paradise and allowed perpetual access to the tree of life, upon condition of obedience to the law that God imposed on him as a test of his loyalty.

In support of this position, I submit three arguments: First based on the laws of hereditary descent already presented against Darwin's theory of evolution. Those who maintain that all men are descended from Adam, are forced to cross the great chasm lying between the several species and types of the animal kingdom upon Darwin's mythical bridge of transmutation of species, or surrender their position. You can no more derive a white man from the African type by the laws of hereditary descent, than you can a dog from a jackal, or a cat from a lion. And it will not do to appeal to the miracles in order to escape this dilemma. For when you do that, you will admit the creative power, which is exactly what we claim was exercise in the formation of each species or type throughout the animal kingdom.

Our second argument is based on Revelation. A critical examination of the Bible history of creation will show two distinct creations of man. One recorded in the first and the other in the second chapter of Genesis I hold that the creation of the inferior types of men is given in the first chapter of Genesis alone with the general account of the creation of the earth and its vegetable and animal kingdoms. While the creation of the Adamic type is reported by a different author and at a later date as given in the second chapter of Genesis is by a different and much earlier writer than the remainder of the second chapter, is evident from the difference in style of the two writers. From the difference of the manner of the creation as reported by each, and especially from the fact that the first writer uses the word "God." While the second calls him the "Lord God." The later writer was evidently a Hebrew and gave an account of the Adamic stock in order to furnish the Hebrew genealogy from Adam through Abraham, down to the times of Moses, while the earlier writer gave the general account of the creation to the advent of Adam. The author of Genesis was simply compiling and placed the two narratives in their natural order and connection. Let us for a moment compare the two creations and the condition imposed on the creation as reported by the respective writers. The manner of the first creation and the laws given for the government of the created, are recorded in twenty sixth, twenty- seventh, twenty- eight, and twenty-ninth verses of the first chapter of Genesis and reads as follows viz: "And God said, let us make man in our own image, after our likeness: and let them have dominion over the fish of the sea, and over the fowl of the air. And over the cattle, and over all the earth, and over every creeping thing that creepeth upon the earth. "So God created man in his own image, in the image of God created he him male and female created he them.

And God blessed them, and God said unto them, be fruitful and multiply, and replenish the earth, and subdue it. And have dominion over the fish of the sea, and the fowls of the air, and over every living thing that moves on the face of the earth, and every tree, in which is the fruit of a yielding seed; to you it shall be meat.

The manner of the second creation and the laws imposes on the created are recorded in the seventh, eight, ninth, fifteen, sixteenth, seventeenth, eighteenth, twenty-first, twenty third, twenty fourth verses of the second chapter of Genesis, and reads as follows, viz: And the Lord God formed man out of the dust of the ground and breathed into his nostril the breath of life; And man became a living soul. And the Lord God planted a garden eastward in Eden; And there he put the man whom he had formed. And out of the ground made the Lord God to grow every tree that is pleasant to the sight and good for food. The tree of life also in the midst of the garden, and the tree of knowledge of good and evil. And the Lord God took the man and put him into the garden of Eden to dress and to keep it. And the Lord God commanded the man saying, of every tree of the garden thou mayest eat. But of the tree of knowledge of good and evil, thou shall not eat of it. For in the day that thou eatest thereof thy surely die. And the Lord God said it is not good for a man should be alone; I will make a helpmeet for him. And the lord God caused a deep sleep to fall upon Adam, and he slept. He took one of his ribs and closed up his flesh instead thereof. And the rib, which the Lord God had taken from man, he made he a woman, and brought her unto the man. Adam said this is bone of my bones, and flesh of my flesh; She shall be called woman, because she was taken out of man therefore, shall a man leave his father and mother, and cleave unto his wife; And be one flesh."

The following distinct differences in the two creations are at once apparent. The first was a general creation like that of the lower animals. The second, a specific creation of the sufficient importance, for the manner and matter of the work to be given. The first was a creation of more than one person, and of both sexes; The second of a single male upon whom was conferred great powers and privileges. The first was commanded to multiply and replenish the earth. To the second no such commandment was given. The first received no charge of business or labor; the second was required to dress and keep the garden of Eden. The first was given dominion over the lower animals; the second was placed in charge of paradise. The first was given the herbs and the fruits of earth for subsistence. The second was given luscious fruits of Eden, and access to the tree of life. The first was left to the ordinary laws of sexual affinity, as other animals. To the second was finally given a helpmeet, and sacred institution of marriage. The first was left associate with and have dominion over the lower animals. The second was accorded the companionship of Jehovah himself as long as he obeyed the laws given him as a test of his loyalty. From the foraging, and many other considerations which might be presented, it is evident that the creation reported in the first chapter of genesis refers to the inferior types of men, who were no doubt, on the earth long prior to Adam.

That there were men on the earth, outside of Adam's family is evident by the fear expressed by the murderer, Cain, that everyone who findeth me slays me."

He certainly did not fear his mother and father and he had already slain his brother, the only remaining member of the family we have any account of then existing. Nobody ever heard of a murderer having fears of posterity. Whom then could Cain have so feared, if there wasn't men on earth outside the Adamic family? He was banished to the land of Nod and soon had a wife and family. Where could he had found a wife, if there was no women in the land of Nod? He soon built a city and name it for his son. How could a city be established without a population? There can be little doubt, that Cain's wife was a Mongolian woman and this city was occupied by the Mongolian people. Eden is conceded to have been in western Asia, where the Mongol Tartars, had probably been leading their nomadic life for thousand of years before. The superior civilization of Cain, who was a tiller of the soil and an architect able to build a city, would naturally attract many of his wife's race to his city in quest of more of the comforts of life.

Again we are informed in the sixth chapter of Genesis, that the immediate cause of the flood and destruction of the Adamic race was its miscegenation with another type of men on the earth.

The sons of "God" who took wives of the daughters of men necessarily refer to the natural sons of God, to be found among the inferior types of men already on the earth before the advent of the Adamic family. Adam's family were called men because of the highest type of man. The entire Adamic race, except the family of Noah and all the mixed stock, was not destroyed by the flood. The historian who records the tremendous events of the flood was no doubt a Hebrew; and in conveying the idea that all men and animals not saved in Noah Ark, were destroyed, simply meant that all the Adamic race except Noah family and all the domestic animals, especially provided by God to Adam, were destroyed, excepting, of course the seed preserved by Noah in his Ark. And as there could have been no reason for destroying the inferior types of men, on other parts of the earth. Who had mixed with the Adamic race, there is no reason to suppose that the flood extended beyond the parts of the world occupied by the Adamic population which would have left the inferior types still existing. As we find then in nearly every part of the earth, with many evidences of their occupancy for a period, extending much farther back into the past than the epoch of the Noachian deluge as us ally computed by the orthodox world.

The wonderful preservation of Noah and his family we believe to have been for the purpose of keeping the earth a pure specimen of the highest type of man. In order that the world might be populated, as it had been, by a great race of progressive and history making nations. And the reason that Noah's family was selected is clearly given. "He was perfect in his generation; that is not mixed with the inferior type and consequently not degenerated "evil in every imagination of his heart" as the race generally is reported to have been.

We now submit our third argument in favor of the creation of the distinct types of men. Based on the data which the most orthodox believer in the unity of the race, cannot dispute. Those who hold

215

that all men are descended from Adam through Noah insist that the flood was universal, and destroyed all the men on the earth except Noah's family.

According to this view, all types of men now found on the earth descended from the three sons of Noah. Now, if I am able to take you to the tenth chapter of Genesis and show where all the sons and grand sons of Noah settle after their dispersion and what races and nations sprang up from them. It should turn out that none of the inferior type of men are found among the descendants of Noah, and then I have established my proposition from the standpoint of orthodoxy.

The tenth chapter of Genesis which locates the sons and grand sons and the races and nations which sprang from them reads as follows, viz:

"Now these are the generations of the sons of Noah and one can read this for yourself.

And we will let you decide for self,

As the poor old negro would say, the writer have taken you the reader to the water but I be dam if the writer can make you drink that derive from choice and the power lies Within that Choice derives from you the reader. The same as the power of any belief any belief share the same power as any, only truth will determined the power of a fact and a fact is built on the foundation of reality.

Thanks for reading this book may peace be upon you.

POST CONCLUSION:

To the writer himself this most daring experience, he has ever experience since the mind is what make the person. The mind has to be in complete total solitude to come up with a conclusion to a thought. It took five Years to write this book, many events have occurred during that time span. But within that time span the writer has experience that time don't change only the events of time the writer can see clearly why unity and strength are part of the same scenario they go together like male and female join together to procreate one can't get no closer than male to female join to procreate, by procreating a new beginning joins the Universe. That is the same when unity and strength don't joined, evil begins the typical American Negro haven't derived at that its seems. That's part of the equation was kept from the poor old Negro, when unity and strength joins together and mate love is procreated. When love is procreated heavens open up love is the only answer, when love is the answer there will be no war, love is so beautiful, love can be compared to the Sun the Sun provides energy. What would the Universe be without the Sun? Imagine if every spirit had love how great the Universe would be there will be no evil, no jealousy no envy, or no hatred every aspect of life would be beautiful just think a life without killing, or envy, there would be no need for war love is all good everyone would love everybody as self no wine o's no drug addicts no one pedaling a belief its all good, for the good love is the answer. Now my friends, that's a dream for the dreamer mathematics has plainly demonstrated that one can't have two answers. That goes to explain the parable in the Bible that one can't serve two master one will love one and hate the other. In essence, what it means one can't love and hate at the same time, it all come under the heading of unity. One cannot have unity with right and wrong in essence, what the writer is saying one cannot choose what to love because god is love, God loves all one will have to choose one cannot love both, that's the law of mathematics. That's the very reason why one must surrender to truth; one cannot be an angel and a devil at the same time. Mathematics do not recognize a split personality, there is only one love meaning there is one unity in essence, mathematics say it can only be one answer. For instance, if Johnny dumb ass has two uncles one uncle is straight and plain, his resume will be the only thing Johnny dumb ass sees from his perception, and his perception is only recognized by himself. now if Johnny dumb ass unravel himself, he would really see how small his perception is. Now on the other side of the spectrum is where the other uncle resides. His resume reads who- who among dumb-ass's it reads as follows: a drunk, a drug addict, a dead beat, a child abuser, a rapist, a jail bird, a procreator of drunks, drug addict, prostitute, jail birds, a menace to this society, and a personal victim to violence. If Johnny dumb ass was for rightness and purity he would unite with the best, that's'goes to explain why Johnny dumb ass didn't unite with education he is just a typical American Negro. A typical American Negro will set back and do nothing, and will have a saying if it was good enough for my daddy it is good enough for me. So, where is the margin for progress when in fact the daddy left the education to the next generation? And by leaving education to the next generation that person is unifying with hope, hope is worthless hope has no value the same as a belief hope is trust in nothing. That is the same as a person that educate themselves it is not recognize by the education department, to be recognized by the education department one must unite with education. By uniting with education, one gains strength and knowledge, just as concrete unite with steel, to become stronger and more durable that comes from education. Education derives from experience, experience is gained from wisdom, and wisdom is experience from yesterday. If it was not for yesterday there will be no today, today is unified with association, association derives from unity, unity paves the way for strength evidently, Johnny dumb ass do not understand that because Johnny dumb ass exist in his world of self existence. And that existence is only recognize by himself and being recognize by only self he do not understand what unity means, and he is a bible toting member. And from that bible he totes the bible say that thru unity there is strength and don't Johnny dumb ass know that if he unite with nothing that nothing will be more stronger than something history has plainly demonstrated that with that first load of Slaves that came to this here America on that Slave ship Jesus. If only the Slaves would had united America would not be known as we know it as we write.

The writer must stop here because we do not want to write a book on Johnny dumb ass, but the writer do want to explain a little bit more about love. A person must have strength

Just to exist to their common task one must have strength just to fight their emotions since the emotions derives from the soul that explain why the typical American Negro is weak, weakness derives from not being united. Why do you the reader think weak people unite with weak people it goes back to the poor old Negro saying birds of a feather will flock together? It all derive from the mind just as Mr. Leonard Bohannon seen clearly that the writer didn't belong on the corner with the wine o's he gave the writer words of wisdom. But, on the other side of the spectrum Johnny dumb ass can't give what he don't have by not having the enlightenment of a bright intellect one don't know that by uniting one will become a combination, a combination is required for strength. History has plainly demonstrated that on that ship Jesus with that strong small combination of dirty ship hands that brought a ship load of wild African to this America; to start what we know now as the typical American Negro.

May Peace be upon you my brothers and sisters until we meet again to be continued:

Jun & Louise DeHorney

writer asked her did she remember how much love he gave her and Mike after their parents abandon them. The writer was program to love them by his mother Josie as if they were the gift of love, but Scharlene and Mike didn't share, the same empathy as the writer. The writer wonders if it was as if they wanted to be very distinct, or was it absolute ignorance we can only wonder. Scharlene and Mike displayed the same empathy, as their formal Slave owner their great-great- grand-father. Who indicated everybody for self, and God for us all, now that is selfishness at its' best. Scharlene and Mike remind the writer of a true story he once heard at church over fifty Years ago as we write. A little nappy head black negro boy while living in Oklahoma saw this blind white woman trying to cross the street although, it was some white folks present but gave her no assistance. The little Negro boy went up to her and asked her ma'am do you need help crossing the street, 'yes I do she replied' So, he grab her by the arm and led her safely, across the street. Once safely across the street, and near other white folks she looked at the little Negro boy and said you get your black, filthy, hands off of me that was her thanks of gratitude she remembered. What the poor old Negro must and cannot forget, they are what they think, and they are the ones who chose what to think and from that choice it develops into a habit, and from that development it becomes their character, and that character is hereditary meaning if they procreate they are programming the next generation in other words, they are programming a cycle. When they program a cycle they are controlling the next generation it all started on that Slave ship good Jesus. The writer mother had a saying, if one want to be successful don't run from love, and don't run to love just to be love it's worthless. It's what one believe that will determine their future the mind is what make the person.

We the writer believe that Coach J. Dehorney can testify to that at one hundred percent.

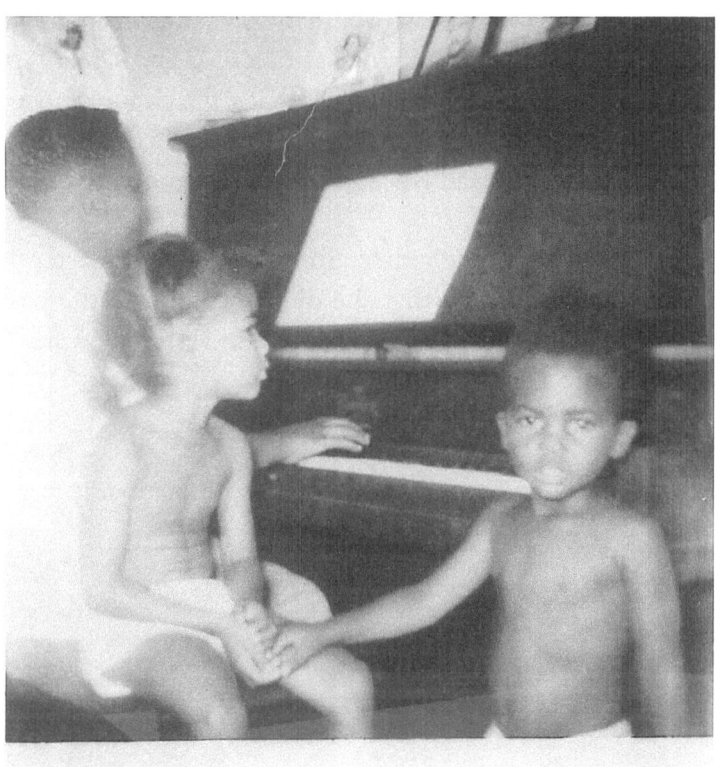

As Etta James song would say at last, we reached the final picture, this is the writer entertaining his niece and nephew Scharlene and Mike. To bring them joy, peace, and happiness that was recommended by the writer's mother Josie for her precious grandchildren. We can only wonder what if? If their mother and father had not abandon them, that enable us to take this picture showing Scharlene and Mike displaying their innateness, that goes all the way back to Africa by wearing few clothes. Scharlene was six years old at the time too old to be in that position, the typical American Negro is a wonderer by nature they can only wonder. The poor old American Negro use if as a conjunction to indicate circumstances, if indicates ignorance. If it was not for if the poor old Negro would not have nothing, and nothing is very empty or absolute. We can only wonder about if, if is very powerful yet, its' only a two letter word but, it seems to be the motto' for the poor old Negro.

The poor old Negro is always wondering, just like the poor old dog that was chasing a rabbit, he stopped to take a #2 and said afterward, if I hadn't stop I could have had lunch. That's' the circumstances that surrounds not knowing, one can tell were life have led lead them, but can't tell where life will lead them, the writer is sure everyone agrees with that.

Scharlene once told the writer, after receiving her master degree at Arizona state University that she didn't hold on to the past and the writer will Quote her "Jun I do not live in yesterday world". that exclamation came after the writer